The Stories Behind Every Song
LED ZEPPELIN
Dazed And Confused

DEDICATION

This book is dedicated to John Henry Bonham – the heartbeat of Led Zeppelin

Published in the United States by
THUNDER'S MOUTH PRESS
161 William Street, 16th Floor, New York, NY 10038

This edition reprinted in 2001

ISBN 1 56025 188 3

Cataloging-in-publication data available from the Library of Congress

Project Editor: Lucian Randall
Copy Editing: Graeme Kidd, Sally Newman
Picture Research: Clive Webster
Production: Alexia Turner

3 4 5 6 7 8

Printed in Italy

acknowledgements

The author would like to thank Howard Mylett, Mel Wright, Phil Carson and
Lucian Randall for their tireless help and assistance.

The Stories Behind Every Song
LED ZEPPELIN
Dazed And Confused
Chris Welch

THUNDER'S
MOUTH
PRESS

"Please welcome LED ZEPPELIN!"

"Christians to the lions!" groans John Henry Bonham, as he grabs his drum sticks and heads towards the roaring crowd that lies in the darkness beyond. The nervy musicians file from the tiny concrete cell that serves as a dressing room, where they have been psyching themselves up for action. Now the practise amps are abandoned as they hurry through dingy corridors patrolled by armed cops with dogs, towards a floodlit stage besieged by fans. This will be their world for the next two-and-a-half hours. While Bonzo climbs aboard his massive drum kit, and Jimmy Page and John Paul Jones take up flanking battle positions, Robert Plant alone faces the yelling throng. He snatches the microphone and shouts back into the far reaches of the cavernous sports hall: "Shut up!"

The indescribable tumult of cheering, whistling and hollering only increases and Robert looks down at the eager, expectant faces in the front rows. "Alright, give us a kiss," he relents. Now they are ready to launch into a spectacular, energy sapping show during which this unique band will play some of the greatest rock epics of all time. 'Dazed & Confused', 'Whole Lotta Love', 'Communication Breakdown', 'Good Times Bad Times'. These are songs that inspire and excite generations of fans around the world.

But the show only scratches the surface of their output. For this is Led Zeppelin 'live', in 1970, young, fresh and dynamic. There is a lot more to come. Tonight the band are on stage in Berlin, Germany. But they could be at Madison Square Garden, New York or the Royal Albert Hall, London. Whatever the venue during their years of heavy touring, Led Zeppelin invariably created magic on stage and received ecstatic welcomes from an ever expanding audience. I was fortunate to be with them during those early days, to see the best rock'n'roll group in the world in action. It was an unforgettable experience. But the story did not end with cheering crowds and broken box office records. Led Zeppelin's most important work was in the studio. Here Page, Plant, Jones and Bonham, working for long hours without distraction and interruption, realized their musical vision. Here they created the songs that would become the staple diet of their stage shows until their split in 1980. Their sources ranged from the unequivocal outpourings of passion drenched in the blues, to revitalized folk songs and titanic rock riffs.

More obtuse concepts, lyrics and melodies, cloaked in legend and mystery were later forged into master works like 'Stairway To Heaven' and 'Kashmir'. Over the ten albums that comprise the Zeppelin legacy, there was a richer variety of songs and styles than most bands could ever envisage. The sheer diversity of their output has since provided a source of endless speculation.

The band themselves always felt that too much explanation of their work and examination of its origins and influences was unnecessary. "Let the music tell its story" was their simple cry. Yet each song undoubtedly has its own special meaning, to the composer, the listener or humble interpreter. A fuller understanding of Zeppelin's aims and intentions, based on observations and information gleaned from a variety of sources, as well as comments the band themselves have made over the years, only makes listening to their records a more satisfying and fulfilling experience.

It is with this in mind that we have attempted to focus on the roots and inspirations of Led Zeppelin's core material. We hope we have cast some light into the recesses of their musical minds. But the more you listen, the more you wonder. There *is* magic here. And to paraphrase The Beatles – where *did* it all come from?

CHRIS WELCH, London 1997

Contents

INTRODUCTION

OVER THE HILLS AND FAR AWAY

When Led Zeppelin burst on the world scene with their debut album in 1969, the reaction ranged from stunned disbelief to incomprehension. The electrifying excitement of 'Dazed And Confused', the menace of 'How Many More Times' and the sheer frantic exuberance of 'Communication Breakdown' were just some of the performances that instantly set Led Zeppelin apart. Here was an album that would redefine and shape rock music for the next 25 years.

Zeppelin would go on to create more classics like the mysterious 'Kashmir' and the world's most famous rock ballad, the magnificent 'Stairway To Heaven'. Few critics could immediately grasp the band's amazing potential, and this led to frustration, controversy and misunderstanding within the tightly knit group. However, there were those who quickly recognized the significance of the forces being unleashed by this dynamic new group. They also realized that Led Zeppelin were not, as the damning press reported, 'The last word in savagery'. Perhaps the wonderfully exaggerated tales of debauchery and mayhem that have grown up around the band's name have contributed to their lasting appeal. After all, it would be an intensely dull bunch of superstars that never threw a TV set out of a window.

Even today, when every last iota of evidence about the Zeppelin years has been chronicled and mulled over, there are still those who wince or flee for the hills at the mention of their name. All nonsense of course. It's true there was a slight risk, during the band's more high-spirited moments, of the unwary being tied up with sticky tape and suspended from a fourth floor office window, or of ending up in a swimming pool having had their trousers ripped off. Even so, the creative spirits who comprised Led Zeppelin were

never mere caricature monsters of rock.

When Jimmy Page first conceived the idea in 1968, his aim was simply to create the best rock group in the business. It was always the MUSIC that was the *raison d'être* for Led Zeppelin; it was true at the time, and it's what keeps their memory so palpably alive now. Nevertheless, the larger-than-life personalities behind the Zeppelin image were crucial, both to their success and appeal.

When the British group first appeared in America on December 26, 1968, they caused a sensation. Girls screamed, boys cheered and other groups refused to play on the same bill.

Jimmy Page, with dark curly hair, satin outfits and knowing smile, seemed like the master of revels, as he raised his violin bow to scrape the strings of a guitar that howled with ecstatic pain.

Robert Plant, poet and blues shouter, contemplates his Zeppelin future

Robert Plant, a mass of golden hair cascading over his shoulders, bare-chested and clad in tight jeans, strutted the stage with a cocky impudence that was irresistible. As he sang from deepest tenor to screaming falsetto his voice was like another instrument, fencing with Page's flashing guitar.

Behind them was the ultimate rhythm machine – John Paul Jones, a warm and melodic bass player, whose forays onto a Hammond organ added an eerie and mysterious tone to many a Zeppelin classic.

John Bonham, drum master and *bon viveur* provided a cataclysmic blast of percussion that not only galvanized the band but inspired their best-known riffs.

Quite early on in their career it became obvious that they weren't just a hard rock riff band. The 'heavy metal' tag was always ludicrously inappropriate, but such was the power of their impact that many a critic, put on the defensive, resorted to abuse.

The legacy of eight studio albums they recorded between the years 1968 and 1979 contains a rich variety of songs and performances that few others can equal. The sheer diversity reveals a band clearly searching for new ideas and keen to experiment. The blues and rock'n'roll were certainly at the core of their work, but the variety of ethnic influences in their songs and ballads shows an intelligent face to the Led Zeppelin of myth and legend. Mysterious music from Middle Eastern deserts and Indian mountains were among the many exotic influences absorbed by chief composers Plant and Page. Soul, funk, folk, country music, West Coast psychedelia, even hillbilly and reggae were all grist to the Zeppelin mill, given their fascination for all aspects of pop music culture.

These elements were judiciously introduced right from the start. From 'Black Mountain Side' on *Led Zeppelin* (1969) to 'Gallows Pole' on *Led Zeppelin III* (1970), from 'Stairway To Heaven' on their untitled fourth album (1971) to 'Kashmir' on *Physical Graffiti* (1975), the group devised a sort of musical alchemy that turned nearly everything they touched into musical gold.

There were few moments when they faltered – compared to most of their contemporaries, their output remained at a consistently high level. Sometimes their delving into traditional blues sources lead to accusations of plagiarism, but that's a game that could be played with the entire history of rock'n'roll. It's perhaps enough to say that before 1968 there wasn't a band that sounded quite like Led Zeppelin.

Led Zeppelin may not have captured the public's affection in the same way as the Beatles or the Rolling Stones, and they may not have been as flashy as The Who or the Jimi Hendrix Experience, but there was a monumental power and strength about the Plant-Page crew that overwhelmed all opposition. They were the record breakers, the biggest concert attraction, the greatest album-sellers, the most talked about band of the 70s. And that's the way Page planned it.

GOOD TIMES, BAD TIMES

Yes, there had been some marvellous British bands in the years before Zeppelin. Jimmy Page's old buddy Eric Clapton had soared to success in the first supergroup Cream. Jeff Beck, another mate from the Yardbirds, had teamed up with Rod Stewart to create a group that held great promise. But when Jimmy Page, aided by manager Peter Grant, set out to launch his own band, he wasn't so much concerned with getting star names, as finding the best performers.

All his own experience, gained over years of touring and session work, would be poured into the new project.

James Patrick Page, (born January 9, 1944) a doctor's son from Heston, Middlesex, England, had studied painting in his youth and quite early on developed an appreciation of antiques and *objets d'art*. But he had also discovered Elvis Presley and rock'n'roll and, once he was given his first guitar at the age of 12, he was hooked on rock and determined to become a professional musician.

His family moved away from the noise of Heathrow Airport to live in Epsom, where Jimmy went to Grammar school. He studied the famous tutor book Bert Weedon's

> QUITE EARLY IN THEIR CAREER IT BECAME OBVIOUS THAT THEY WEREN'T JUST A HARD ROCK RIFF BAND.

Play In A Day and had a few guitar lessons. But he largely taught himself by listening to solos on records by his favourite artists, particularly Elvis Presley's 'Baby Let's Play House', and the guitar work of Scotty Moore. James Burton was another favourite and Page appreciated the acoustic work of British folk artist Bert Jansch. In 1958 Jimmy formed a skiffle group that veered towards R&B and began playing at local clubs. He also made an appearance on BBC TV's *All Your Own* hosted by Huw Wheldon. Rare black and white footage exists of his interview, which shows a well-spoken, intelligent lad already displaying a sense of independence.

He may have looked like 'a little shrimp', as his mate Jeff Beck called him, but there was always a steely strength of purpose about Jimmy. At the age of 15 Page left school and plunged into the rock life, quickly moving to London, where he visited all the clubs and sat in with band leader Cyril Davies. His first pro job was with singer Red E Lewis and The Red Caps, then he joined Neil Christian and The Crusaders in 1959. But he found the life on the road, living in a van and bed-sits,

debilitating, and after a bout of glandular fever, he concentrated more on session work in the studios.

Recommended by engineer Glyn Johns, Jimmy played on his first session, which was 'Diamonds' (1963) by Jet Harris and Tony Meehan, both of whom had recently left the Shadows. His first work in the studio resulted in a No. 1 hit! He also worked with pop group Carter Lewis and The Southerners, and pictures of him at this period show a sharp-looking young Mod with a friendly smile. Between 1963 and 1966 he played on countless sessions. Among the huge variety of artists and bands he worked with were Van Morrison and Them, The Who, the Kinks, Donovan, Chris Farlowe, Lulu, PJ Proby, Mickie Most, the Bachelors, Val Doonican, Burt Bacharach and Cliff Richard.

PAGE WOULD OFTEN BE CALLED IN AS 'INSURANCE' BY PRODUCERS WORRIED IF THEIR STAR BANDS COULDN'T CUT IT IN THE STUDIO.

Sometimes he'd play solos, or simply fill in with rhythm guitar. Page would often be called in as 'insurance' by producers worried if their star bands couldn't cut it in the studio. This sometimes led to friction in the studios as regular band members resented having this unknown young expert on their sessions. Jimmy grew used to getting daggers looks, but his anonymity spared further embarrassments.

For many years Page remained a shadowy figure, well respected within the music business, but not nearly as well known as the more flamboyant Eric Clapton and Jeff Beck. Eventually, Jimmy grew tired of being asked to play on 'Muzak' sessions and wanted to become part of a regular group playing his kind of music. As Jimmy recalls: "Working in the studios certainly gave me a sense of discipline and at the same time I developed different styles of guitar playing. I was also very keen on finger-style acoustic guitar playing, but towards the end of my session period I was playing less featured stuff and just strumming along, and I got fed up with it. It was time to go and it so happened that's when the Yardbirds opportunity turned up."

Page had been asked to join the band before – when Clapton left – and had refused. But he relented finally and joined the Yardbirds in 1966. Jeff Beck was

Jimmy Page – buttons up his overcoat

Pop star PJ Proby
used sessionman
Page on his albums
and singles

still the band's lead guitarist, and Jimmy came in on bass guitar. This situation developed because the band's regular bassist, Paul Samwell-Smith, had abruptly quit after a huge row. Recalls Page: "We'd always wanted to play together and suddenly the opportunity was there. I took over the bass for a while, until the rhythm guitarist (Chris Dreja) had learned the bass, and then Jeff and I could play lead guitars."

After rehearsing for two hours, Page went off with the Yardbirds on a full American tour. The pressure of heavy touring led to Beck undergoing fits of rage and depression. Sometimes he wouldn't turn up for a gig, so Jimmy took over. Other times Jeff and Jimmy would work together as a dual front line, creating a deafening wall of stereo sound that threatened to blow away the frail Keith Relf. It was very exciting but it caused tension. Eventually Jeff decided to quit the band in 1968.

Jimmy became the Yardbirds' last lead guitarist, although he was rarely seen in this role in Europe, as the band concentrated on working in the States. The Yardbirds were highly influential, and had been very popular in their heyday, but were undergoing a severe decline. Exhausted and demoralized by heavy touring and a lack of chart success, the band decided to split. They broke up after a gig in Luton, Bedfordshire, in July 1968.

Page was encouraged by the Yardbirds' last manager, Peter Grant, to form his own band and plans were laid to recruit new members. Jimmy had been writing songs, experimenting with new techniques and was now keen to try them out in the studio. The original plan was to bring in singer Terry Reid and drummer BJ Wilson from Procol Harum to help form what would be known as the New Yardbirds. Chris Dreja was briefly retained from the old group and session pianist Nicky Hopkins was also involved, until session bass player and organist John Paul Jones (real name John Baldwin, born June 3, 1946, Sidcup, Kent) called Jimmy, having heard he was getting a band together.

Reid and Wilson turned down the project. Terry had just signed a solo recording contract and couldn't come in, but he recommended a young singer from the Midlands called Robert Plant instead...

Robert (born August 20, 1948) in West Bromwich, had been known as 'The Wild Man Of Blues From The Black Country' and had been singing with such groups as the Delta Blues Band and the Crawling King Snakes. Plant grew up listening to authentic American blues artists, and through singing in local club bands, he soon developed his own immensely powerful and passionate vocal style. By the time he'd joined his last pre-Zeppelin outfit, the Band Of Joy, he'd spread his wings to embrace everything from blues to hillbilly and soul. He'd released a brace of solo singles under his own name for CBS in 1966/67, but without any commercial success. Robert

Plant was a star waiting to be discovered.

The Band Of Joy boasted an unusually loud and aggressive drummer called John Bonham (born May 31, 1948, West Bromwich), who had previously worked with Robert in the Crawling King Snakes. In 1968 the band, with Plant and Bonham, toured the UK, backing American artist Tim Rose. Clashes of temperament ensured there would always be a lively atmosphere within the band – indeed, there was a full-scale fight among the musicians one night when the drummer suggested a new billing: 'The Band Of Joy featuring John Bonham.'

Jimmy and his manager Peter Grant went to see Robert singing with a group called Hobbstweedle at a gig in Birmingham. Jimmy was blown away by Robert's voice and couldn't believe he hadn't already been spotted. The singer was invited to come to London right away and he agreed, after recommending his old mate 'Bonzo' Bonham for the drummer's job.

Jimmy went to see Bonham playing with Tim Rose, and recalls that it took ages to get Bonham to agree to join the new band, because Bonham felt he had a 'steady' job with Rose's group. Page persisted: "...he was exactly the type of powerhouse drummer I was looking for! Eventually we got the four of us into one room and that was it. We just exploded." The New Yardbirds, as they had to be called for contractual reasons, were complete and ready for a ten-day tour of Scandinavia that had already been booked for September, 1968.

Page expected the youthful enthusiasm of his new partners to ignite the band's inner fire. He wasn't disappointed. When the feisty four found themselves playing in a cramped rehearsal room in Soho for the first time, the pent up energy was unleashed as they tore into 'Train Kept A-Rollin''. "It was powerful stuff!" remembers Plant.

Soon after these first rehearsals, their debut album was recorded in days rather than weeks. Manager Peter Grant had moved with similar speed to get the band work. On October 15 they made their UK debut at Surrey University under their new name – Led Zeppelin. Apparently Jimmy Page had considered calling the band the Mad Dogs but, as he later commented, "The name wasn't as important as the music. We could have called ourselves the Vegetables or the Potatoes. I was quite keen about Led Zeppelin as it seemed to fit the bill."

The name Led Zeppelin had derived from the dire predictions of The Who's Keith Moon and John Entwistle that the new enterprise would go down like 'a lead balloon'. They couldn't have been more wrong. The new band arrived at a perfect time. British rock was in limbo with the demise of many excellent bands, yet there was a growing market not just for live bands, but for albums. Club gigs were being replaced by three-day festivals and PA systems were growing ever larger. The age of the one-hit-wonder pop group was over – at least for a while – the age of Stadium Rock was dawning and Led Zeppelin was ready for action.

> ## PAGE PERSISTED:
> "... HE WAS EXACTLY THE TYPE OF POWERHOUSE DRUMMER I WAS LOOKING FOR! EVENTUALLY WE GOT THE FOUR OF US INTO ONE ROOM AND THAT WAS IT. WE JUST EXPLODED. "

The Yardbirds in 1967

Keith Moon and John Entwistle of The Who said Page's new band would "Go down like a lead balloon – or a lead zeppelin!"

While other bands were let down by a poor singer, a recalcitrant drummer, or a temperamental guitarist, Led Zeppelin were super strong in all departments and thrustingly confident. Robert Plant had been waiting to show the world just how fiendishly well he could sing. Classically trained John Paul Jones desperately needed to express his own talents beyond the realm of the studio. John Bonham was a one-man powerhouse. His sheer volume and bombastic style meant few bands had

properly exploited him. And Jimmy Page was bubbling with brilliant ideas: songs, arrangements, sound effects, production and showmanship.

While the new band launched into their early gigs at colleges and small clubs, Peter Grant, the ex-all-in-wrestler and movie actor, was using all his strength and ferocious personality to win the band a record contract. Eventually they signed to Atlantic Records in New York City for $200,000. It seemed like a lot of money at the time.

ZEPPELIN LIFT OFF

The debut album *Led Zeppelin* was recorded in October 1968 and released in January 1969 in the States, and March in the UK. The group had already made their first American concert appearance in Boston, on December 26, 1968, where they caused a sensation and blew US bands Iron Butterfly and Vanilla Fudge off stage.

Now the world could hear the recordings that have since become part of the soundtrack of a generation: 'Good Times Bad Times', 'Babe I'm Gonna Leave You', 'You Shook Me', 'Dazed And Confused', 'Your Time Is Gonna Come', 'Black Mountain Side', 'Communication Breakdown', 'I Can't Quit You Baby' and 'How Many More Times'. Nowadays, following 25 years of advances in studio technology, these tracks might not seem as dynamic as they did in 1969. However, in the context of the often messy, sloppy and poorly mixed productions of the period these original recordings were a revelation.

Re-mastered versions of Zeppelin's classic tracks have since revealed new depths and hidden subtleties. Yet the vinyl album, for all its microscopic flaws, has an intriguing atmosphere that can never be reproduced. Only The Who's original *Tommy* double album has the same kind of mysterious quality of sound. It was that sound – and the brash enthusiasm of the bubbling new band – that caught the imagination of the lucky few who heard advance review copies of *Led Zeppelin*.

Early in 1969, at *Melody Maker*'s untidy Fleet Street office, Tony Wilson, a young, new reporter, rushed into the editorial department clutching a 12-inch vinyl album. Its striking cover showed the famous news picture of the Hindenburg airship crashing in flames at Lakehurst New Jersey, in 1937. It was an eerie enough image – part cataclysm, part phallic symbol. Somehow the notion of sex and explosions registered before a note was played. Tony had seen Led Zeppelin at the Marquee Club and was convinced they would be the biggest band of the new decade – "Listen to this – you gotta hear Robert Plant's voice."

That early Marquee show had only attracted a few hundred people. Most were shocked by the battering volume and were unfamiliar with material that seemed to be the blues, but was played with a ferocious intensity that was almost indecent to audiences more used to the earnest warblings of John Mayall & His Bluesbreakers.

The apparent indifference of the crowds at early British shows was disappointing. As Jimmy Page recalls: "It wasn't until we got to America that the audiences went wild. They didn't know what had hit them." Within a year English fans were also yelling with all the enthusiasm of their American counterparts.

There had been earlier clues about what to expect from this untried band. They had all served as session men on an album by P.J. Proby, the Texan pop singer who had located to London during the 60s and become a local hero. Proby had caused a sensation with hits like 'Somewhere' and his trouser-ripping antics, but his last album *Three Week Hero* (1969) had passed unnoticed. If anybody had bothered to listen to a track called 'Jim's Blues', they would have heard Robert Plant wailing on harmonica. During the track the pent-up, hungry-for-action Zep men threatened to blow Proby out of the studio. It was a dress rehearsal for an album now being previewed at radio stations and in magazine offices around the world.

Led Zeppelin were not just The New Yardbirds. This was a stunning blast of brash performances in which the drums thundered, the organ wailed, the guitar rushed like a tempest and the singer seemed on the verge of exploding. This was the album that would set in motion a career full of drama, excitement and a scale of success unimaginable to young musicians who had been struggling for a living wage, let alone a millionaire's fortune.

TEN YEARS GONE

When Zeppelin first hit the road at the end of 1968 they were still very much a four-piece rock band in a station wagon with a roadie. Robert Plant was still doing the PA mix from the stage using a tiny old 150-watt amplifier he'd owned in the Band Of Joy. Even when they played prestige gigs like the Fillmore, San Francisco their PA sound was pretty primitive. But the sheer power of the newcomers soon overwhelmed competition such as Country Joe & The Fish.

This was something more explosive than the Woodstock Generation had ever experienced. Word spread across the States like wildfire and everyone wanted to see this newest example of the British invasion. Page, Plant, Bonham and Jones became mega rock stars and the endless cycle of tours and recordings continued for a turbulent decade.

There were the great events – Bath Festival (1969), Carnegie Hall, New York (1969), Madison Square Garden, New York (1970), Earls Court, London (1975) and Knebworth, England (1979). Their albums and singles dominated the charts, and by the end of their first year together it was said they'd already earned some $5 million in sales.

Although singles were discouraged by the band's management at home in England, it didn't stop them having hits in America like 'Whole Lotta Love' (1969), 'Immigrant Song' (1970), and 'Black Dog' (1972). Even 'D'yer Mak'er' (1973), 'Trampled Under Foot' (1975) and their 1980 opus 'Fool In The Rain' made it into the US Billboard Top 40. Led Zeppelin rapidly became even bigger than Elvis or the Beatles in terms of sales, and each album was eagerly awaited by millions of fans.

WORD SPREAD ACROSS THE STATES LIKE WILDFIRE AND EVERYONE WANTED TO SEE THIS NEWEST EXAMPLE OF THE BRITISH INVASION.

Led Zeppelin II (1969) topped charts around the world and yielded 'Whole Lotta Love' and 'The Lemon Song'. Then came *Led Zeppelin III* (1970), *Four Symbols (Untitled)* (1971), *Houses Of The Holy* (1973), *Physical Graffiti* (1975), *Presence* (1976), *The Song Remains The Same* (1976), *In Through The Out Door* (1979) and the final release *Coda* (1982). The band were voted best in the world in the 1970 *Melody Maker* Readers' Poll and stayed at the top for a decade. As they toured the world they were greeted with riots and uproar. At a single concert at Tampa Stadium, Florida in May 1973, they played to over 56,000 people and grossed $309,000.

In 1974 the band expanded their business activities, setting up their own label 'Swan Song' and signing their favourite artists like the Pretty Things and ex-Stone The Crows singer Maggie Bell, who was managed by Peter Grant. A party held in Chislehurst Caves to launch the label's releases became a byword for excess and debauchery as scantily clad girls danced "a light fandango and turned cartwheels across the floor."

In 1975 the band were at a peak of popularity when they played spectacular three-hour shows for five consecutive nights at London's Earls Court arena and performed thrilling material from *Physical Graffiti*. They used a 70,000-watt PA system and a complex lighting rig – a far cry from the early days when Robert's battered old amplifier provided the driving force. Performances of 'Kashmir' and 'Trampled Under Foot' caused a sensation remembered by fans to this day, and it was the same story throughout their American tour that year. Zeppelin flew around the States on their own chartered 'Starship' and provoked riots at the box offices as tickets sold out within hours of going on sale.

The group capped their achievements when they starred in their own movie. *The Song Remains The Same* premiered in New York in October 1976. The movie showed the band in concert and was interspersed with so-called fantasy sequences that revealed each member of the band indulging in what might have been their own personal fantasies. John Bonham raced a drag-strip car, Robert Plant rescued a fair maiden from a castle, John Paul Jones appeared as a masked night rider, while Jimmy Page climbed a Scottish mountain on the shores of Loch Ness in total darkness, in search of a mysterious Hermit. Manager Peter Grant later called it "the most expensive home movie ever made", but it was a big success at movie theatres around the world.

As they broke box office records during these years of marathon US tours and platinum albums, the band was increasingly plagued by controversy, mainly fed by lurid stories in the teenage rock press. Certainly the band exhibited high spirits. John Bonham was seen riding motorcycles down hotel corridors, while rooms were trashed and redecorated with hamburgers and ketchup. Half-naked groupies were pressed into nightly service amid the shattered piles of broken furniture.

But the real culprits were the road crew and not the band. John Bonham may not have been an innocent bystander but certainly Robert Plant and Jimmy Page were nowhere near this kind of action. They were far too cool to indulge in such stunts. On the road, the band were often quiet and reserved, worried about the next gig, the flight or simply yearning to get home to their respective families. Robert Plant was usually seen on planes and buses, quietly reading magazines or listening to tapes by Joni Mitchell. Away from the gig or hotel Jimmy Page went about collecting antiques at local flea markets or studying ethnic music forms. Even John Bonham usually preferred a pint of real ale with his mates to indulging in exotic antics with dubious creatures of the night.

Speculation about Zeppelin's secret goings-on remained rife, but the true turn of events proved much more dramatic. Mishaps like Robert Plant's car crash on the Greek island of Rhodes in 1975, during a family holiday, when he and his wife were seriously injured, certainly cast a shadow over the band's success.

ZEPPELIN'S LAST STAND

Robert recovered sufficiently from his car crash injuries to take part in recording sessions at Musicland, Munich, for the album *Presence* (Swan Song), which was released in April, 1976. Although not up to the standards of *Physical Graffiti*, it yielded one blockbuster, the amazing 'Achilles Last Stand'. In the same year they released their double-soundtrack album from *The Song Remains The Same*, packed with Zeppelin classics, including live versions of 'Rock And Roll', 'Dazed And Confused' and 'Stairway To Heaven'.

Everything seemed to be going their way when, in April 1977, the band set off on their 11th tour of the US, which would be their biggest ever. On April 30 they played to 76,229 fans at the Pontiac Silverdome, which broke another attendance record. Yet clouds were gathering... There was a riot at Tampa, Florida

when a show was cancelled because of a storm. A six-night stint at Madison Square Garden went without incident. Then backstage at the Oakland Coliseum, a minor dispute sparked off a backstage fight between members of the Zeppelin crew and the promoter's security men. This resulted in arrests and criminal charges for assault. Worse was to come.

A few days later, on July 26, a message came from England that Robert's young son Karac (five) had been taken ill with a stomach infection. He was taken to hospital but was dead on arrival. Robert flew back to England and the tour was cancelled. In the light of such tragic events it seemed unlikely that Robert would sing or the band would play for a long time.

It was a dark time for the band, but life had to go on. Later that year, with Robert sufficiently recovered from his emotional trauma, Led Zeppelin got back again to begin the final stages of their career. In May they reunited to make music together at Clearwell Castle, in the Forest Of Dean. It was the best kind of therapy.

During December 1978, the revitalized band went to Sweden and recorded *In Through The Out Door* at Polar Studios, Stockholm. In June the following year they embarked on a new European tour and, on August 4 and 11 1979, they topped the bill at two sensational shows held at Knebworth, England. In September *In Through The Out Door* was released and topped the US charts, selling over four million copies in America alone.

During April 1980, the band began rehearsing in London for what would be their last European tour and announced plans to return to North America. On July 7 they played a concert in West Berlin, then in September met up at Jimmy Page's home in Windsor to rehearse for the US tour. Perhaps worried about the impending return to the States, Bonham embarked on a vodka-fuelled drinking bout. On Thursday, September 25 John was found dead, having suffocated on his own vomit. His funeral was held on October 10, 1980. Fans around the world were stunned by his death, as tragic as the loss of his contemporaries Jimi Hendrix and Keith Moon. Tributes poured in, many from his fellow drummers

BONHAM'S DEATH WAS A SHATTERING BLOW THAT PRECIPITATED THE BREAKUP OF THE GROUP.

Opposite:

John Henry Bonham –

drummer

who saw Bonham as both an idol and a pioneer of heavy rock.

Bonham's death was a shattering blow that precipitated the breakup of the group. In December the band issued a bleak communiqué which said: "We wish it to be known that the loss of our dear friend and the deep sense of undivided harmony felt by ourselves and our manager, have led us to decide that we could not continue as we were."

As Jimmy Page confirmed, this meant the band could not continue to work as Led Zeppelin without John Bonham. In the aftermath the remaining members seemed unnerved by all that happened. Their fans were left disappointed and crushed by the loss of the greatest rock band they'd ever known. All they had left from the debris was a 1982 album of Zeppelin relics called *Coda* barely advertised and relegated to the bargain basement bins within weeks of release.

Such was the hostile mood of the early 80s to the previous decade's heroes, that it was uncool even to mention their name. Robert Plant was the first to recover. He began to rebuild his career with a commendable zeal and a bright new image, releasing a succession of solo albums and touring with his own bands. Jimmy Page, after a period spent in seclusion, recovered his nerve and strength, wrote some film music and performed at charity shows and low-key gigs before taking the plunge and forming The Firm in 1985, with former Free vocalist Paul Rodgers. Page later worked in a touring band that featured John Bonham's son Jason, now an excellent drummer, and the singer John Miles.

Fans yearned for a full scale Led Zeppelin reunion and there were some historic moments – like Jimmy's moving performance of 'Stairway To Heaven' at London's Royal Albert Hall during the ARMS charity show in 1983. This was also the occasion when Jimmy, Eric Clapton and Jeff Beck joined forces on stage for the first time ever. As the decade wore on, new bands paid their dues to the group that had inspired them in their youth. Zeppelin's music was re-evaluated and, while music critics were still wearing punk-rock attitudes on their sleeves, artists were sampling Led Zeppelin, copying their riffs and covering their numbers in a wave of adulation that reached a peak with the bizarre Dread Zeppelin.

Zeppelin watchers were constantly kept busy. There were several collaborations between Page and Plant, including the Live Aid show at Philadelphia's JFK Stadium on July 13, 1985, with Phil Collins on drums, and the Atlantic Records 40th birthday celebrations at New York's Madison Square Garden, in May 1988, when Robert sang 'Stairway To Heaven' and 'Whole Lotta Love', backed by Jason Bonham.

In June 1988 Jimmy released his first solo album *Outrider* and toured with Jason and John Miles. Then came a brief liaison with Whitesnake singer David Coverdale, for the album *Coverdale/Page* (1993) which resulted in just one tour of Japan. It seemed a strange choice to work with Coverdale, who had been criticized by Robert Plant for being a Robert Plant clone. Was it a ploy by Jimmy to encourage Plant to return to the fold where he belonged? If this was so, it certainly worked. The long-awaited reunion finally took place in 1995 when the pair recorded the sensational *Unledded* MTV show followed by a hugely successful Plant-Page world tour.

Without John Paul Jones or the late John Bonham, it could not be Led Zeppelin, but it was the closest fans would ever get to the real thing restored to former glory. The songs of their youth retained their mystique and power to entrance. 'No Quarter', 'The Battle Of Evermore', 'The Rain Song', 'When The Levee Breaks', and the extraordinary 'Kashmir' were all revitalized and it was undoubtedly the happiest and most convincing work either had done in years. Despite all they had been through, the magical chemistry between the two men clearly remained the same.

But where did it all come from – that mysterious outpouring of sounds and ideas first captured on eight extraordinary albums? What were the influences, the circumstances, the people and events that sparked Zeppelin's creative flame? Perhaps the 'where' is not so important as the 'how'. And this is how it all began...

> ...ARTISTS WERE SAMPLING LED ZEPPELIN, COPYING THEIR RIFFS AND COVERING THEIR NUMBERS IN A WAVE OF ADULATION THAT REACHED A PEAK WITH THE BIZARRE DREAD ZEPPELIN.

1 LED ZEPPELIN I

LED ZEPPELIN (ATLANTIC K40031) 1969

Exploding across the scene with a barrage of blues: *Led Zeppelin* was an astonishing debut album. It still retains its capacity to shock and excite nearly 30 years later.

GOOD TIMES, BAD TIMES

BABE I'M GONNA LEAVE YOU

YOU SHOOK ME

DAZED AND CONFUSED

YOUR TIME IS GONNA COME

BLACK MOUNTAIN SIDE

COMMUNICATION BREAKDOWN

I CAN'T QUIT YOU BABY

HOW MANY MORE TIMES

essions for the debut album took place during October 1968 at Olympic Studios, Barnes in West London, where many bands from the Rolling Stones to the Nice had recorded.

Engineer Glyn Johns recalls that the album took about nine days to record and the band were only actually in the studio for some 30 hours, at a cost reputed to be a mere £1,782. However, the power and spontaneity of these performances can be put down to the fact that the band had already been rehearsing and touring before they arrived at Olympic. As Glyn explains: "It was a very exciting record to cut."

Page adds more detail: "The group had only been together for two-and-a-half weeks when we recorded it! We'd had 15 hours rehearsal before shooting over to Scandinavia for a few gigs, then straight after that we cut the album. There was very little double-tracking. We were deliberately aiming at putting down what we could actually reproduce on stage."

Page's ideas. concepts, guitar solos and effects dominate the album. As he said: "It was obvious somebody had to take the lead. But everyone was inspired. Everyone was a star. There wasn't any weakness there. Everyone was strong."

He introduced sounds that hadn't been heard before, sounds that have since become part of the language of rock. "I had a strong idea of exactly what I wanted to do on the album, which involved using a lot of contrast that I didn't think anybody else was doing."

"I wanted to get an ambient sound and I also had this idea for using backwards tape echo, which I suggested before on a Yardbirds track. So I knew it worked! I also wanted there to be a lot of light and shade and a certain dramatic tension. I know that I influenced pretty heavily the content and arrangements but that was only because we didn't have the time to discuss everything between us. The first album was a real mixture of blues, rock and acoustic music."

Each track had a life and purpose of its own but blended together in a way that seemed to create what is known in classical terms as 'programmatic music'. Led Zeppelin wasn't just a string of tunes – it was a complete experience.

GOOD TIMES, BAD TIMES

Like a pounding fist clamouring for attention, Page's guitar chords herald the first few seconds of Zeppelin magic on a song that encapsulates the band's style. Here are all the elements that make them special; the interplay between guitar and vocals, the use of breaks to create dynamic tension, and the rumbling aggression of the drums used as counterpoint to the action.

Behind Page's opening shots Bonham can be heard building the tension, first with his closed hi-hat, then with tentative tinkles on the cowbell, before the snare drum explodes behind Plant's vocal debut.

"In the days of my youth I was told what it was to be a man!" he howls. "Good times, bad times." Then a split second of pregnant silence is superseded by a shattering burst of notes, like machine gun fire, from Page's guitar. Bonham's right foot dances on the bass drum pedal with an unheard of dexterity. It caused many a young drummer sore ankles as they tried to emulate the effect. John Paul Jones' impish bass breaks momentarily hold Plant back from his vocal climax: "I don't care what the neighbours say, I'm gonna love you – each and every day!"

Although ultimately an inconclusive performance, this group composition, with its catchy refrain, was at one time considered worthy of release as a single. Peter Grant, however, always voiced his opposition to the concept of singles as he felt they detracted from album sales, a policy that dazed and confused the record company on many occasions.

> **" I KNOW THAT I INFLUENCED PRETTY HEAVILY THE CONTENT AND ARRANGEMENTS BUT THAT WAS ONLY BECAUSE WE DIDN'T HAVE THE TIME TO DISCUSS EVERYTHING BETWEEN US. "**
>
> JIMMY PAGE

Led Zeppelin celebrate signing their Atlantic Records contract in 1968

For this opening cut, Page used a Fender Telecaster guitar put through a Leslie Speaker cabinet, normally used with the Hammond organ, which helped attain a distinctive swirling tonal effect. For the rest of the time he used a minuscule amplifier with a 12-inch speaker, which belied the enormous power he seemed to generate throughout the sessions. The tune was played on early gigs but later deleted from the 1970 medley built around 'Communication Breakdown'.

BABE I'M GONNA LEAVE YOU

hen Plant first visited Page at his house by the Thames, during the summer of 1968, they sat playing albums by their favourite artists to gauge each other's musical tastes. They listened to everyone from Elvis Presley to Muddy Waters and Joan Baez.

'Babe I'm Gonna Leave You' was a Baez album cut that particularly appealed to Page, who had long been interested in folk music of all kinds. He'd played this behind Marianne Faithfull during his session days and it was one of the first numbers that Page suggested to Plant might be worth covering.

Page's arrangement of the piece turned into a dynamic performance which quickly established the band's commitment to using both electric and acoustic modes. The result was certainly a far cry from heavy metal. It turned into a beautifully crafted performance filled with shifting moods and intriguing effects.

Launched by a simple guitar introduction, Plant breathes "Baby, baby, I'm gonna leave you" – a gentle restraint that is suddenly replaced by a voice full of anger and menace, as the band roars behind him to create a dramatic re-enactment of the theme. The mixture of power and control shown here is remarkable. As Plant's voice bids a discrete farewell in the final bars, it is a chastening thought that so little rock music has since attained anything like the standards of sophistication set here.

"It has a very dramatic quality," says Page who is still very proud of this arrangement. Although the band believed 'Babe I'm Gonna Leave You' was a traditional song, (it had also been recorded by Quick Silver Messenger Service), it was later discovered that it had been written by composer Anne Bredon, a 60s folk singer, who was later given an appropriate credit on the *Remasters* set of Zeppelin albums.

YOU SHOOK ME

Originally composed by blues man Willie Dixon and previously recorded by Muddy Waters, the song had also been covered by Jeff Beck on his 1969 album *Truth*. This produced some complaints from the Beck camp in the light of Zeppelin's later success. In the event, this was a real Zep blockbuster, on which Plant gives a bravura performance. Squabbles about who did what first should not detract from the overall achievements on a remarkable first album.

The blues was a kind of open house in the UK at the time, when bands like John Mayall's Blues Breakers, Fleetwood Mac and Stan Webb's Chicken Shack were all attempting to recreate Black American music with, it has to be said, far less exciting and satisfying results. Zeppelin's confident treatment of the source material ran rings around their competitors.

This track is a real low-down dirty blues in which Plant's harmonica practically spits out his feelings. The use of a glissando in which voice and guitar slide in sexy unison is a masterstroke, and you can hear a burst of laughter behind Plant's vocals which show how much everyone in the studio was obviously enjoying themselves.

John Paul Jones excels with double-tracked solos on electric piano and organ which, in the words of Ian Dury, are very funky indeed. Plant's extended harmonica solo is interrupted by an outburst of tom tom fury from the

drummer, then Page begins a solo which is illuminated by a heart-stopping guitar break, creating one the most celebrated moments in Zeppelin lore.

Another great call-and-response sequence follows when the vocalist and guitarist embark on a kind of pitched battle, before 'Bonzo' Bonham brings everyone safely back down to earth with a few well-chosen claps of bass drum thunder. Heavily featured on their early tours, the number was eventually elbowed aside as more original works dominated the band's live set.

Folk singer Joan Baez. Her version of 'Babe I'm Gonna Leave You' appealed to Jimmy Page

Jimmy bow wows the fans at Bath Festival, 1970

DAZED AND CONFUSED

Undoubtedly the *piece de resistance* and an astonishing work by any standard. 'Dazed And Confused' was the performance that convinced first-time listeners that here was a band in the throes of making rock history. Most can remember where they were and what they were doing the first time they became conscious of those subtle, doom-laden notes, ushering in a truly magical arrangement.

Listeners were barely recovering from 'You Shook Me', when John Paul Jones' bass guitar spilled into the next track. Conceived by Page, the basis of this arrangement had first been performed by the Yardbirds, during their final days in America. The piece had its origins in an acoustic tune known as 'I'm Confused' that had been performed in the 60s by New York folk singer Jake Holmes. A version of the song appears on his 1967 album *The Above Ground Sound Of Jake Holmes*. Page is believed to have heard him perform it during a visit to New York.

Led Zeppelin's treatment had new lyrics and, like all the best arrangements in classical music, it developed a life and personality of its own. The tune became a staple of live concerts and was frequently extended into a 40-minute showcase, during which Page played his guitar with a violin bow. (This innovative technique was used as a gimmick by guitarist Eddie Phillips, who played with British band Creation in the London clubs during the mid-60s. Creation recorded two singles, 'Makin' Time' and 'Painter Man', which were produced by Shel Talmy for the Planet label in 1966. Both have become collectors' items.) Some concluded that Page's use of the bow had been inspired by Creation, but he later revealed that the idea had come from a fellow musician, during one of his many pre-Zeppelin recording sessions. "I just wanted the guitar to sound different," he explains.

The idea was suggested to him, in fact, by actor David McCallum's father, a session violinist who met Page, was impressed by his playing and asked if he'd ever considered attacking the guitar with a violin bow. Page thought this would be difficult because the violin had a specially arched neck while the guitar neck was flat. But he tried it out with astonishing results. In Page's hands the bow became not only a symbol of showmanship, but a magical device, creating extraordinary sounds never heard before. He used the technique with The Yardbirds, Led Zeppelin and his 1985 band The Firm.

'Dazed And Confused' is a *tour de force* in which the use of eerie silences, the funereal walking bass and spine-tingling notes create an unforgettable atmosphere. Howls greet Plant's angry tale of woe as the band engage in a weird four-way conversation. Bonham impatiently speeds up the tempo, while Page's guitar spatters forth an appropriately confused barrage of notes. Then the return to a slower tempo is both haunting and menacing. This closes the first side of a vinyl album that packs in more brilliant ideas than would be evident in many another band's entire recording lifetime.

> **" I JUST WANTED THE GUITAR TO SOUND DIFFERENT. "**
>
> JIMMY PAGE

YOUR TIME IS GONNA COME

Credited to Page and John Paul Jones, this gave Jones a chance to show off his abilities on the church organ, while Page made use of a Fender pedal steel guitar. Played on the band's early dates in Scandinavia, the song was later dropped from the show.

Jones uses bass pedals on the organ to fill out the sound, until Plant begins to protest at the woeful lack of courtesy shown by the modern girl. "Lying, cheating, hurting, that's all you ever seem to do," he grumbles. But although she drives him insane, one day her time is gonna come and she'll find him gone. The pedal steel that Page uses to accompany this verbal onslaught is slightly out of tune, which adds to the strangely plaintive air that persists until Bonham's sternly bashing drums bring a sense of direction to the final chorus. Part of this song was sometimes used on the band's 'Whole Lotta Love' medley.

BLACK MOUNTAIN SIDE

though only two minutes long, this little gem epitomizes the tasteful, intelligent approach adopted by Page while wearing his two hats as producer and guitarist. It was considered quite daring to introduce an 'instrumental' into the middle of an album intent on establishing a new band, in which key members, including the highly-prized lead vocalist, were excluded. But why not? The interlude afforded by this showcase for Page's finger-picking acoustic guitar work only makes the subsequent return to all four cylinders the more effective. The piece actually starts well before the end of 'Your Time Is Gonna Come' and once again it is one of those little unexpected engineering touches that still delights and intrigues the first-time listener.

Page's repeated figure – played on a Gibson acoustic guitar – sets up a drone matched by the sensuous tabla drums played by Viram Jasani, a respected Indian musician who continues to work and broadcast in Britain. This piece was influenced by the Yardbirds' 'White Summer' which Page recorded with them. Others attribute it to the Bert Jansch tune 'Black Water Side'. Page often played it during Zeppelin tours, as a showpiece in a medley with 'White Summer', when he sat down on a stool and attempted to quieten the audience down to listen. It was partly incorporated in performances with The Firm and his subsequent band.

During the performance on the album he employed what he dubbed a special 'CIA tuning', meaning it contained Celtic, Indian and Arabic influences. This DADGAD tuning would also be employed on 'Kashmir' from *Physical Graffiti* and elements of this tune would later be heard on the Firm's 'Midnight Moonlight'.

COMMUNICATION BREAKDOWN

ommunication Breakdown baby!" The vision of a screaming Plant, tossing back his mane of golden hair and shaking his legs with more energy than a brace of Elvis Presleys, became an enduring image of the 1970s. "What fun!" as Plant would say.

Hard on the heels of 'Black Mountain Side' this thunderous workout quickly became one of the most popular Zeppelin concert riffs, even though it was, in retrospect, technically the least interesting performance on the album. It was first heard during their early tour dates in Scandinavia during late 1968. Released as a single in the US in March 1969, coupled with 'Good Times Bad Times', it became something of an anthem, only rivalled by 'Whole Lotta Love', from Led Zeppelin II.

Taken at breakneck speed, this early example of a Plant-Page composition is pure rock'n'roll, built around a hammering guitar riff, delivered by Page in the spirit of Eddie Cochran. It was hard work to play, but the song remained in the band's set for many years either as a show opener or as a special encore. There were periods when it was dropped in favour of new material.

Essentially it's a piece of high spirits designed to free audiences from conformity. Plant's lyrics sum up the teenage angst of the tongue-tied and frustrated. "Suck it" he yells just before a ferocious guitar solo.

I CAN'T QUIT YOU BABY

n outstanding performance, this interpretation of a Willie Dixon tune was one of the highlights of the album, and of many a Zeppelin show. A simple blues it made comical most other British and young American bands', attempts to interpret the black idiom.

The vision of a screaming Plant, tossing back his mane of golden hair and shaking his legs with more energy than a brace of Elvis Presleys, became an enduring image of the 70s

But it was more than a bash through a 12-bar. It was a loving exploration of a theme, with all its attendant nuances. Page excels as he answers Plant's initial vocal remarks with unpredictable guitar mutterings that leave spaces interspersed with Les Paul-ish blips, splutters and then beautifully constructed phrases.

This contrast between perfection and imperfection is daring and effective. It's the stuff of living music that no machine could emulate, and is what gives these Zeppelin recordings their unique quality. John Bonham's bass drum snaps like a jack hammer, but he plays the merest touch on his Ludwig metal snare drum, showing that he was also capable of restraint and good taste.

HOW MANY MORE TIMES

How many more times!" yelled fans at Bath Festival when the band played there in 1969. To the uninitiated it seemed as though the audience were complaining. In fact they'd already turned on to Led Zeppelin and were desperate to hear the final explosive item from the album.

It swings into action with another irresistible walking bass line from John Paul Jones that sweeps everything before it, like the roar of a jumbo jet's engines at cruising speed. But beyond the riffs, this piece develops into an extraordinary farrago of freak-outs, in which elements of ideas culled from past Yardbirds and Band Of Joy sessions were combined into one devastating arrangement.

The use of a bolero rhythm pushes the piece towards a frantic climax, followed by Bonham's tom toms answering eerie groans from the guitar. Page had produced Jeff Beck's 'Beck's Bolero' earlier, but this idea was only part of a much broader spectrum. Plant's finest vocal moments come when he develops the chant of "Oh Rosie, steal away now" over a New-Orleans-style snare drum rhythm, and slots in more vocalists in-jokes, including a quote from 'The Hunter'. The engineer uses his knobs to pan the sound for a crash, bang and wallop finale to this spontaneous eight-minute studio extravaganza.

Portrait Of The Artists As Young Men

2 LED ZEPPELIN II

(ATLANTIC 588 198 RE-ISSUE K40037) 1969

Led Zeppelin II had huge advance orders. It sold three million copies within months of its release in October 1969 and soon topped both the US and UK album charts.

WHOLE LOTTA LOVE

WHAT IS AND WHAT SHOULD NEVER BE

THE LEMON SONG

THANK YOU

HEARTBREAKER

LIVIN' LOVIN' MAID

RAMBLE ON

MOBY DICK

BRING IT ON HOME

ed Zeppelin were incredibly busy throughout 1969 as they consolidated their grip on increasingly hysterical audiences throughout America. Their concert schedule also took in trips back to Europe, which meant they had to write and record their keenly-awaited second album at odd moments in different studios. Despite these difficulties, they achieved what many thought might prove impossible. When *Led Zeppelin II* was finally released, it easily matched the dynamic excitement and explosive power of their debut album.

The year had begun with the band playing at Bill Graham's Fillmore West, in the heart of hippie San Francisco, during the first week in January. They supported Country Joe and The Fish, though it's likely that Country Joe felt he'd been slapped around the face with a red snapper by the time Page, Plant & Co had finished their set. The response was incredible. Fans screamed in ecstasy and even formerly sceptical rock critics hailed them as "the best British band since Cream and the Jimi Hendrix Experience".

When Zeppelin moved on to the East Coast and played at New York's Fillmore, they virtually destroyed another band they were supposed to be supporting. Iron Butterfly, hitherto hailed as the nation's heaviest band, retreated in disorder, and by all accounts never fully recovered from the experience.

At first Zep were playing for a mere fistful of dollars, but by April the money had shot up and their box office ratings increased. Zeppelin now topped the bill at both Fillmores and, during their third US tour of the year, they found themselves playing at such unlikely events as the Newport Jazz Festival and the Schaefer Music Festival in Central Park, New York.

Everyone wanted to see Led Zeppelin and the band were naturally thrilled at the response. In between gigs, their hotels proved a haven for rest, recuperation and high jinks of every description. After reaching a spiritual and physical high during a concert, it was expecting a lot for them to return to their rooms and quietly watch the TV weather forecast. It was much more fun to greet the horde of young lady admirers who flocked to enquire about their well-being. On one occasion, the story goes that Page was delivered to a waiting throng of girls on a room service food trolley, greeted by shrieks of delight. On another occasion

John Bonham and his sidekick, tour manager Richard 'Ricardo' Cole, enjoyed themselves riding motor cycles. One of the eyewitnesses to this event was Scots singer Maggie Bell, who was also managed by Peter Grant, having previously sung with Grant protégés Stone The Crows.

As Bell recalls: "Bonzo and Ricardo were celebrating the purchase of a boat. They had a huge Hollywood party that went on all day, and I remember them riding these motor cycles around the lobby of the Hyatt House, on Sunset Strip. They called it the Riot House by the way. Alex Harvey, the Scottish bandleader, was staying in the same hotel and he got really annoyed that they were making such a racket playing records. He shouted at them out of the window above their rooms: 'If you don't turn that noise off I'll come down and sort you lot out – NOW!' And they all went deathly quiet because they were actually frightened of him."

Bell was also present when the band's manager, Peter Grant, made his famous offer to a hotel manager. "The manager came in and said 'It must be great to have so much fun trashing a room. I've always wanted to do that.' Peter took out his wallet, gave him $2,000 and said: 'Here, be my guest. Go wreck a room.'" The manager agreed that Led Zeppelin weren't such bad guys. He told his British guests: "We had the Tabernacle Choir here last week and they were much worse. They completely wrecked the joint!"

Virtually overnight, the band, that only months before had been living in bedsits and scraping a living, had become affluent superstars. Their excesses were largely tolerated since they were enjoying the first flush of success, but there was much serious work to be done.

During the round of flights, hotels and concerts, recording sessions were snatched in Los Angeles, New

> **" THE MANAGER CAME IN AND SAID 'IT MUST BE GREAT TO HAVE SO MUCH FUN TRASHING A ROOM. I'VE ALWAYS WANTED TO DO THAT.' PETER TOOK OUT HIS WALLET, GAVE HIM $2,000 AND SAID: 'HERE, BE MY GUEST. GO WRECK A ROOM'. "**
>
> MAGGIE BELL

York and London. Most of the mixing sessions took place at A&R Studios, New York, under the auspices of engineer/producer Eddie Kramer, who had worked with Jimi Hendrix on the *Electric Ladyland* album.

Page later described the scattered recordings sessions as "quite insane". They had to write many of the numbers in their hotel rooms and backstage, and he began to develop nagging fears that the second album might be fatally flawed as a result. There was no need to panic. *Led Zeppelin II* when it finally appeared in the US on October 22, 1969 turned out to be a blockbuster. As the band's attorney Steve Weiss put it: "Jimmy – the new album is a masterpiece." Weiss was right. The album was brilliant. It had a life and quality all of its own. The strange almost ghostly atmosphere that pervaded the first album was replaced by a tougher, brasher sound, but there were moments of inspired madness that seemed to link both records.

Led Zeppelin II had huge advance orders of half a million copies in the US alone, and in its first week of release, leapt to No. 15 in the US charts. Zeppelin soon beat even the Beatles' *Abbey Road*. and *Led Zeppelin II* went on to top the album charts in the US and the UK, selling three million copies within a few months.

> **" NONE OF US EXPECTED IT TO BE THAT BIG. IT WAS A TOTAL SHOCK WHEN I HEARD IT WAS SELLING FASTER THAN THE FIRST ALBUM. IT WAS RATHER FRIGHTENING, THE WAY IT SNOWBALLED. "**
>
> JIMMY PAGE

"None of us expected it to be that big," said Page. "It was a total shock when I heard it was selling faster than the first album. It was rather frightening, the way it snowballed."

The vinyl album's cover, with artwork by David Juniper, is now one of the most familiar in the gallery of rock art. Against the band's Hindenburg logo is pictured a group of what look like Hell's Angels, but are in fact German air aces from the First World War. Closer scrutiny reveals four familiar visages superimposed on the faces of the leather-clad pilots. The inner gatefold design, showing an airship caught in blazing searchlights above a temple of rock, is pure 30s triumphalism in the spirit of film director Busby Berkeley.

Here are the songs that helped define heavy rock for future generations. From the opening blast of 'Whole Lotta Love', to the thunder of tunes like 'Heartbreaker', the second Zeppelin adventure is packed with pleasures and delights. It remains one of rock music's finest achievements.

WHOLE LOTTA LOVE

ost bands would die to have an anthem as strident, confident and effective as Zeppelin's most famous *cri de coeur*. Perhaps it is not so much a cry from the heart as a yell from the pit of the stomach. Certainly it caused a sensation on first hearing and swiftly became the band's most in-demand show buster, remaining a theme instantly associated with their memory.

Page's celebrated opening riff, both menacing and combative, spurred on by the combined forces of Bonham and Jones, gave Plant a platform for his spectacular whoop. Matching Joe Cocker's roar at the end of 'With A Little Help From My Friends', Plant's prolonged outburst of "Woman you need l-o-o-o-v-e" was forceful enough to reach the moon.

'Whole Lotta Love' was recorded at Olympic Studios under the auspices of engineer George Chkiantz and later mixed in New York by Page and Eddie Kramer. The main theme is contrasted by a lengthy improvized section. In edited form it was released as a single in the US, backed with 'Living Loving Maid'. It shot up to No. 4 in December 1969 and spent 13 weeks in the Billboard chart; the song was also No. 1 in Germany and Belgium.

It seemed destined to be a big hit in Britain too, and no doubt would have been but for one unexpected glitch: Peter Grant didn't want Led Zeppelin to release any singles in the UK. Atlantic Records in London were stunned. When they pressed up copies and tried to put them out, Grant stopped them.

His reasoning was that releasing singles would only harm album sales, a complete reversal of corporate

thinking both then and now. But if people wanted 'Whole Lotta Love' so much, they'd have to buy the LP. It all made sense when sales of *Led Zeppelin II* zoomed through the roof, turning Gold and then Platinum. Peter Grant's apparently arbitrary decision had worked.

The object of all this furore opens with a faint laugh and a yell of "Baby I'm not foolin' … I'm gonna give you my love!" Each one of Plant's exultant statements is greeted by a glissando from the guitar and is set against a sonorous jungle rhythm. Page explained later that the descending groan on his guitar was produced

by judicious use of a metal slide on the strings and some backwards tape echo.

After some minutes of relentless thunder, the mists of sound part to reveal a new soundscape dominated by an eerie tinkling of temple bells. This is produced by Bonham's prudent use of drum sticks on the centre of his cymbals, while his hi-hat (that foot-operated mechanical device which keeps time) stomps out an insistent echoing beat that is full of foreboding. A spooky interlude develops that is more truly psychedelic than anything to be found on Pink Floyd's albums.

"Love!" gasps Plant as Bonham breaks in with a

Plant, Page and Jones receive a gold album for *Led Zeppelin II*

battering assault on his snare drum. Page snaps back into consciousness, his guitar steaming into a riff ... "L-O-O-O-O-V-E!" Boom, crash, pow – the spell is broken.

There never was a real ending to 'Whole Lotta Love' and maybe it should have finished a chorus earlier than the final fade-out. Nevertheless, it is a brilliantly evocative piece of work that is more than just a template for the heavy metal that followed in its wake. The freak out section was worked up in the studio during a free-form engineering session by Page and Eddie Kramer. Explained Kramer: "It was a combination of Page and myself twiddling every knob known to man."

> **"IT WAS A COMBINATION OF PAGE AND MYSELF TWIDDLING EVERY KNOB KNOWN TO MAN."**
>
> EDDIE KRAMER

'Whole Lotta Love' was later recorded by Plant's old mate Alexis Korner (the father of British Blues), with his big band outfit known as CCS. It was part of a rock'n'roll medley and the 'Whole Lotta Love' section was used for many years as the signature tune of BBC TV's *Top Of The Pops*. Interestingly CCS also recorded a respectable version of Page's 'Black Dog' on their 1972 album. It seemed like the session men were paying tribute to one of their old studio colleagues.

Years later, it was suggested there were some similarities between this Zeppelin master work and the Willie Dixon composition 'You Need Love'. The band were sued in 1985, when Dixon's daughter noticed a resemblance. Willie said he first heard the Zeppelin tune in 1983, many years after the band's record had been released.

Dixon (born July 1, 1915, in Vicksburg, Mississippi) was the composer of such blues standards as 'Hoochie Coochie Man', Wang Dang Doodle', 'My Babe', 'Spoonful', 'You Can't Judge A Book By The Cover' and 'The Red Rooster'. All of these became part of the language of rock and provided the staple diet of many of the revivalist British blues bands of the 1960s, notably the Rolling Stones and, of course, all the groups that Page and Plant had played in. Many of Dixon's songs were originally recorded by Muddy Waters, including 'You Need Love' (1962).

Dixon (who died in 1992) was one of the band's heroes, and after his case with Zeppelin was settled out of court, he used the proceeds to help others. He set up the Blues Heaven Foundation to promote awareness of the blues and buy young musicians instruments at schools in Mississippi.

Although Zeppelin have sometimes been criticized for not always fully crediting their use of America's musical heritage, their records furthered the cause of the blues by introducing blues and traditional themes to new audiences. In so doing they promoted many artists who might otherwise have languished in obscurity. Certainly Zeppelin's productions bore little resemblance to the small band recordings made by the pioneers in the 1940s and 1950s.

'Whole Lotta Love' became an integral part of Zeppelin's set, provided a big finale and it was regularly included in their rock'n'roll medley. It was played at such historic latter day events as their 1979 Knebworth concerts, the 'Live Aid' reunion on July 13, 1985 and at the Atlantic Records' 40th Birthday Concert, New York in 1988.

WHAT IS AND WHAT SHOULD NEVER BE

ecorded with George Chkiantz at Olympic Studios, Barnes, and mixed at A&R in New York, this was one of Plant's first compositions to be aired by the band. "And if I sing to you tomorrow", is his opening line as he promises to take a cherished companion for a walk to a castle. Plant's romantic streak and love of myths and legends provided a perfect contrast to the hot-blooded stallion image of the lusty blues shouter. It showed a gentler, more intellectual side to his nature. Even so, the song retains a strong rock section during which Plant returns to a few of his trademark "baby, baby" yelps.

Page plays a solo that owes something to Les Paul, the daddy of electric guitar. Phasing on the vocals,

achieved by the art of engineering, gives a shimmering effect, while the guitars pan disturbingly from the left- to right-hand channels. With drums absent from this touching scene, only a shimmering gong reminds us of the brooding presence of Bonham.

The song, taken at a relatively slow and measured pace, was first publicly performed at the Lyceum Ballroom, in The Strand, London on October 12, 1969. The event coincided with the anniversary of a real Zeppelin attack by German airforces who bombed the building in 1915.

THE LEMON SONG

o should we care about "influences"? The blues is an international language, utilized by countless bands and artists over 50 years of recording and live performance. It would be difficult now to trace who first sang "I woke up this morning" and as for "Squeeze me baby, until the juice runs down my leg" … well similar sentiments can be heard on an Indian pop song complete with sitars, which contains the line "leaky, leaky, down my leg."

Chester Arthur Burnett, better known as Howlin' Wolf (born 1910, died 1976), famed for his recordings of 'Smokestack Lightning' and 'Killing Floor'

And yet for some reason – probably their sudden and devastating success – Led Zeppelin were constantly being sniped at by nit-pickers and probed by musicologists. The band were careless in crediting their sources of inspiration, but if this album had sold three copies in a junk shop, nobody would have noticed references to Howlin' Wolf's 'Killing Floor' during 'The

Lemon Song'. Ever the blues enthusiast, Plant sings this line at one point. Although first listed as a band composition, later pressings credited Chester Burnett (Howlin' Wolf) as the true composer after representations by the publishers.

The average record buyer was happy simply to be swept along with the excitement created by this shameless outburst. Recorded at Mystic, Los Angeles, it was notable for the 'real' echo the studio produced. There is something of the Yardbirds about the way 'Lemon Song' revels in guttural guitar lines. When it lunges into a double-tempo section, Page solos at full tilt over three choruses of blistering improvization. He's still wailing when the band begin to slow down in perfect synchronization; a difficult feat for any band, but expertly done by Bonham and Jones. "Take it down a bit" instructs Plant as he launches into a blues rap. It's a real club performance, light years away from the strictly-controlled musical environments of the 90s.

"The way you squeeze my lemon, I'm gonna fall right off the bed," squeals Plant. To a generation of prudes unused to such sexual innuendo, it all seemed very shocking, and doubtless caused many raised eyebrows in the offices of British radio producers. A spunky dialogue between guitar and vocals follows, then a swift return to frantic tempo.

THANK YOU

One of the most remarkable aspects of Zeppelin's performance on this particular track is not so much what they play, but what they leave out. For a band damned for its supposed excesses, 'Thank You' shows both good taste and the exercise of restraint. It is also one of the best vocal performances by Plant thus far into Zeppelin's recorded career. From his opening statement: "If the sun refused to shine I would still be loving you", this outbreak of deep-rooted sincerity continues to permeate a ballad enhanced by John Paul Jones' mellifluous Hammond-organ tones. Acoustic guitar floats over a wandering bass guitar line and there is a distinct West Coast cool about the vocal harmonies.

With audiences hyped up to expect maximum rock

from their favourite band, it took a while for them to accept such soft, romantic material. But for those ready to listen, here was evidence of the band's expanding horizons. "If the mountains crumble to the sea – there would still be you and me," breathes Plant as a church organ provides a delicate pedal figure that fades away … then returns for a brief reprise. Zeppelin could be justly proud of what is virtually an orchestral arrangement which features one of Page's finest acoustic guitar solos.

Dedicated to Plant's wife, 'Thank You' marked the singer's move towards greater involvement in lyric writing. It was recorded at Morgan Studios, London, with engineer Andy Johns, and later mixed in New York by Eddie Kramer. Featured on stage from late 1969 onwards, it was heard during the January 1970 British tour, when it became something of a keyboard showcase for John Paul Jones. Although still popular in the early 70s, it was eventually dropped from the act.

HEARTBREAKER

Side two of the original vinyl album proved rather uneven after the sustained brilliance of the first tour tracks. 'Heartbreaker', along with 'Ramble On', was certainly among the highlights. Recorded and mixed at A&R Studios, New York, this was a Plant, Page, Jones, Bonham effort that featured one of Page's most memorable outbursts. More than just a 'guitar break', it was a sonic attack that has stayed sharply defined in the memory of fans. 'Heartbreaker' begins with a repeated figure that sounds oddly like "Darn, darn, darn, a da-darn" – a savagely intense set-up for Plant to make one of his grand entrances. "Hey fellows have you heard the news!" he announces. It's time to head for the hills to

An acoustic set was always an essential part of Zeppelin shows from their earliest days

avoid one of these dangerous wenches who break the hearts of men and boys with their flirtatious ways.

'Heartbreaker' shows Zeppelin applying great skill to the arrangement. Plant is never drowned out. When it's time for him to sing, apart from a rumbling bass and guitar accompaniment, he is allowed free rein to bellow from the rooftops. There is none of the constant battling for space that mars the works of lesser bands who fail to understand the need for silence and rests.

The guitar punctuates Plant's vocal lines, then comes one of those nail-biting, cliff-hanging moments when Led Zeppelin stops dead in its tracks. Page sounds an echoing warning blast on his guitar. At live shows, this was invariably the signal for an outburst of expectant cheering from the fans. Harsh, angry, spluttering, furious, the notes cascade from his axe. Drums and bass return as Page solos at full speed. Climax is piled upon climax until another abrupt halt, and Plant returns to continue his diatribe.

"You abused my love a thousand times!" he protests. "So go away Heart Breaker!" The song became a firm favourite at gigs from October, 1969 onwards and was sometimes used to open the set, along with 'Immigrant Song'. Later it was employed as part of a medley of Zeppelin standards. During the live performances, Page expanded the guitar solo and employed bits of other tunes including 'Greensleeves,' and Bach's 'Bourée in C minor' which is not nearly as 'Bourée' as it sounds.

'Heartbreaker' Page solos at maximum speed

LIVIN' LOVIN' MAID (SHE'S JUST A WOMAN)

Zeppelin playing a radio-friendly pop song? Well this is the closest they ever got to that during their career. It's got a real 60s feel and might have been designed for the Merseybeats.

Page, asked what were his favourites, once said that it would be easier to cite his least favourite track: 'Living Loving Maid'. Maybe it's the way the band chorus "DOWN!" as Plant sings "You'd better lay your money down!" Either way Page wasn't keen, but it is still a catchy, attractive melody with some fine country guitar work. It certainly provides a cheery contrast to all the blues rock angst.

Released on the B-side of 'Whole Lotta Love' in the US it later became an A-side in its own right, when it managed to reach No. 65 in the US Billboard chart after extensive radio plays. The song about a groupie "with the purple umbrella and the fifty cent hat" was rarely played live. Plant sang the first line after the band had finished playing 'Heartbreaker' at a gig in Hamburg, Germany in March 1970, and later performed it during his own band's Manic Nirvana tour of 1990.

"You abused my love a thousand times!" roars a testy, chesty Plant

RAMBLE ON

Leaves are falling all around – time I was on my way!" More quality writing from Plant emerges on this track, full of phrases like: "I smell the rain and with it pain." A simple enough rhyme, but strangely telling.

Plant's lyrical flowering was inspired by an acquaintance with the works of JRR Tolkien, author of the celebrated trilogy, *The Lord Of The Rings*, with its tales of elves, dwarves and magic, once astutely described by *The Independent* newspaper as "a comprehensive counter myth to the story of the twentieth century". Many a pop person came under Tolkien's spell in the early 1970s, including the dear, departed Marc Bolan. Not everyone was enamoured by his writings however. Tolkien's friend and fellow author CS Lewis was once heard to complain "Not another fucking elf".

Even so there may well be elfish influences here. Certainly there are magical touches from John Paul Jones' nifty bass guitar, and John Bonham forgoes his trusty Ludwig kit to patter away on his knees with pixie-like pazzazz. When he brings on the drums, he employs the forceful energy that might be expected from one of those Middle Earth creatures, bent on battle with Sauron the Dark Lord.

Bass and guitar engage in a subtle dialogue as Plant embarks on his briskly paced narrative. "I'm gonna ramble on around the world," he muses. Ever the wanderer, Plant once described how a man could take a walk along a street and then turn either left or right and completely change his future life. Tempting. After a multi-track splurge of vocals, there is a very long fadeout, best heard on headphones. Recorded with Eddie Kramer in 1969 at Juggy Sound Studios in New York, 'Ramble On' was never performed live.

MOBY DICK

Led Zeppelin were singularly fortunate in their choice of drummer. John Bonham had all the right stuff, including gusto and an indomitable spirit. He always wanted to put his own stamp on the drums in a way that matched his no-nonsense personality. However, right from his days with Midlands outfits like the Band Of Joy, there were grumbles about his bombastic approach and the sheer volume of his playing. "I got black-listed and barred from all the clubs in Birmingham," he once told me. "I was so keen to play, I'd play for nothing. But I played the way I wanted. 'You're too loud – there's no future in it' they used to say. Nowadays you can't be loud enough!"

For all his bluff exterior, Bonham could be a surprisingly shy and modest man. He was always very conscious of his need to deliver the kind of power Zeppelin demanded night after night on tour. His was the most physical role, and yet his drumming was not all about brute strength – as careful listening to his playing on 'Dazed And Confused', 'Ramble On' and any number of Zeppelin's more sophisticated pieces will confirm. He had perfect control of his snare drum, could utilize cymbals and gongs to create different tones and had quite a jazzman's feel for syncopation and big-band-style phrasing.

Plant's lyrics flowered after he read Tolkien

His foot control over the bass drum pedal was remarkable and he produced an enormous sound on a relatively small kit. He was a carpenter and builder by trade. "Drumming was the only thing I was ever good at," he admitted.

He began playing at the age of five, using a bath salts container and a coffee tin. He progressed to the kitchen cookware before he was finally given a real snare drum at the age of ten. He didn't own a complete kit until he was nearly 16. "It was almost prehistoric. Most of it was rust, but I was determined to be a drummer as soon as I left school," he told me.

As a teenager he was a bit of a Teddy Boy (Britain's fashion-conscious rockers of the 50s), and his first band, Terry Webb and The Spiders, wore purple jackets and bootlace ties. A year later he joined A Way Of Life and, at the age of 17, married Pat, the girl he met at a dance at Kidderminster. He promised to give up gigging and settle down, but the call of the drums was too strong and his next job

was with Steve Brett and the Mavericks, followed by the Crawling King Snakes – where he met Plant – and later the Band Of Joy.

Bonham quickly developed his style and, although his influences included Carmine Appice of Vanilla Fudge, Ginger Baker and, to an extent, Buddy Rich, there is absolutely no mistaking the sound of the man from Worcestershire. Bonham's extended concert solos were always a pleasure to behold, so it was a great shame that 'Moby Dick', his showcase on *Led Zeppelin II*, was undoubtedly a let-down. For some reason it just never took off, and didn't capture the excitement he normally generated on stage.

He needed the adrenaline created by the band to push him into action, and this solo sounds suspiciously like it was recorded in isolation and then dropped into the otherwise encouraging riff that Page sets up for him (a riff so catchy it was used as a theme tune for a BBC 2 TV show). Bonham stops before he really gets started, and launches into a hand drum

John Bonham's 'Moby Dick' showcase drew blood when he played drums with his bare hands

solo on the snare drum and tom toms. This sort of thing often drew blood on stage and was visually very exciting. In the studio it sounded flat. Even when he switched to sticks, the sound was dead and lacking in ambience.

Recording took place at Mirror Sound, Los Angeles, where Bonham built up a respectable roar with a crescendo of triplets, but he only relaxed when Page returned for the final bars. An edited version of his original solo, it should have been entirely re-recorded.

On the road Bonham developed 'Moby Dick' into a 20-minute extravaganza, sometimes utilizing kettle drums. The crowds cheered, the critics made notes and the band disappeared round the back for a quick fag and a sandwich. Plant would re-emerge just as Bonham was taking his bow, and present the exhausted, blood-and-sweat-stained percussionist with a banana.

By the mid-70s Bonham adopted the 'Out On The Tiles' theme to replace his well worn 'Moby Dick'. Plant once observed: "Bonzo always said he was the greatest drummer in the world. When we heard him play, we knew he was!"

> ## " BONZO ALWAYS SAID HE WAS THE GREATEST DRUMMER IN THE WORLD. WHEN WE HEARD HIM PLAY, WE KNEW HE WAS! "
>
> ROBERT PLANT

BRING IT ON HOME

When Robert Anthony Plant was a teenager, his greatest preoccupations were girls, football and music. Although his parents and teachers rather hoped he'd become a chartered accountant, music began to dominate his life and he became caught up in the great skiffle boom that swept Britain during the late 1950s. Learning to play harmonica, kazoo and the washboard, before long Plant was skipping lessons to form groups.

He was particularly attracted to deep country blues and listened to artists like Memphis Minnie, Bukka White and Skip James, also listening to Willie Dixon, Muddy Waters and Buddy Guy. Plant first heard records by the legendary Robert Johnson when he was 15, and was thrilled by the emotion-packed Johnson style, in which vocal lines are alternated with the guitar. It would leave a lasting impression on the young British singer whose own powerful voice had begun to develop apace.

He gained his first experience singing at the Seven Stars Blues club in Stourbridge, Worcestershire, where he played harmonica with the Delta Blues Band. His father, a civil engineer, used to drop him off at the club where he'd happily roar away on 'Got My Mojo Working' to the local, somewhat earnest, blues enthusiasts. But it was the traditional country blues that Plant recreated on 'Bring It On Home'. The slow drag tempo and echoing harmonica evokes a land much deeper south than Stourbridge. Plant even adopts a kind of toothless vocal style set to an authentic guitar accompaniment.

This plaintive interlude is rudely interrupted by the full Zeppelin mob bursting in through the studio doors. Together they conspire to produce a great heavy rock riff that is full of mystery and menace. Then, having sated their musical appetite, the band disassembles down to Plant and Page once more. As the harmonica fades to a squeak you can almost imagine the teenaged Plant rushing to meet his Dad for a lift home from the club.

Scholars now claim the piece was influenced by Sonny Boy Williamson's version of 'Bring It On Home'. Although played live quite extensively in the early days of the band, when Page and Bonham indulged in a drums and guitar duel, it was later used as an encore or incorporated into a link between 'Celebration Day' and 'Black Dog.' Whatever the origins, 'Bring It On Home' gave a timely reminder of the inescapable links between rock and the blues when most thought it had all begun with the Dave Clark Five and Herman's Hermits.

Sonny Boy Williamson toured with The Yardbirds in the early 60s, long before Jimmy joined the band.

Sonny Boy Williamson (1899-1965), a brilliant harmonica player and one of Plant's blues heroes

3 LED ZEPPELIN III

(ATLANTIC 2401002 RE-ISSUE K50002) 1970

Led Zeppelin were still a force to be reckoned with on stage. But their third album was to showcase a more gentle, acoustic side to them, years before doing an unplugged set became popular.

IMMIGRANT SONG

FRIENDS

CELEBRATION DAY

SINCE I'VE BEEN LOVING YOU

OUT ON THE TILES

GALLOWS POLE

TANGERINE

THAT'S THE WAY

BRON-Y-AUR STOMP

HATS OFF TO (ROY) HARPER

A mood of blissful euphoria seemed to break over the rock community during the summer of 1970. Before the death of Jimi Hendrix cast a pall, hippie idealism appeared to have formed a working alliance with a hugely successful music industry. Rock was booming. Millions throughout America, Britain, Europe, Australia and Japan were hungry for all the latest sensations that a remarkable cultural flowering had to offer. There were so many great new performers to discover – the Beatles and Bob Dylan had set the standard and there followed such diverse rock talents as Joni Mitchell, Crosby Stills and Nash, The Who, Santana, The Doors, the Grateful Dead and, of course, Led Zeppelin.

The group began 1970 surrounded by controversy. During a trip to Copenhagen they were unexpectedly threatened with legal action by Eva von Zeppelin, descendent of the airship inventor who loudly proclaimed: "They may be world-famous but a couple of shrieking monkeys are not going to use a privileged family name without permission." The group simply called themselves the Nobs for their night in the Danish capital. Page recalled that Eva von Zeppelin came to a TV studio in an attempt to stop them performing. They managed to calm her down by turning on the charm, but when she caught a glimpse of their LP cover showing the Hindenburg crashing in flames, she was again annoyed. Said Page: "I fled!" He also later refused to take part in a stunt where he was required to fly in an airship over the Alps. "That would be tempting fate," he responded.

After an American tour in April, the sheer pressure on their health and sanity took its toll. Robert Plant collapsed from exhaustion and, in May, both Plant and Page quit the road for a while to escape the madness. They set off for a holiday that would become famous as the source of their third album and the inspiration for much of their new musical direction – one that would shock their fans and their critics alike.

As Page recalled: "Robert suggested going to a cottage in Wales that he'd been to with his parents. It was a beautiful place and I was keen to go there." They set off, accompanied by some roadies (presumably there to fetch water and hew wood). Armed only with their acoustic guitars, a dog and a supply of food and drink, they settled into Bron-yr-Aur cottage by the River Dovey. Legend has it that Bron-y-Aur means 'Golden Breast' and is a poetic description for the way the morning sun fills the surrounding valley. The initial intention had been simply to get away from the hubbub of cities like Los Angeles and New York, and soak up the country vibes of peace and quiet. "We spent evenings around log fires, with hot pokers being plunged into cider," Page recalls. "As the nights wore on the guitars came out and numbers were written. It wasn't planned as a working holiday but some songs did come out of it." One of these immortalized the cottage's name and, consequently, led to much debate about its spelling, with Welsh linguists drawn into heated discussions about the placing of hyphens and the correct pronunciation. Plant eventually bought the place when he found it derelict.

On their return from Wales, Plant and Page reunited with Jones and Bonham and began recording at Headley Grange, a country house in Hampshire, where they hooked up with the Rolling Stones' mobile studio. During June 1970 the band visited Iceland, the land of ice and snow, an experience which had quite a profound effect on Plant.

Then, on June 28, they played at the Bath Festival, England in front of a 200,000-strong crowd. They played for over three hours and won five encores. A bearded Jimmy Page wore a bizarre yokel's country hat and a long overcoat that appeared to have been bought at an Oxfam shop. Robert Plant, in a floral shirt, looked like a Viking warrior on a peace mission, while Bonham wore a purple vest that clashed hideously with his bright green drums. As the crowd gave them a standing ovation Plant told them: "We've been away a lot in America and we thought it might be a bit dodgy coming back. It's great to be home!"

The band kicked off the late afternoon show with the new 'Immigrant Song'. Without the benefit of stage lighting to create an atmosphere it took a while to warm up the vast crowd, many of whom sat lolling on the grass, thumbing through their programmes and eating

> **" THEY MAY BE WORLD-FAMOUS BUT A COUPLE OF SHRIEKING MONKEYS ARE NOT GOING TO USE A PRIVILEGED FAMILY NAME WITHOUT PERMISSION. "**
>
> EVA VON ZEPPELIN

ice cream. But once Page brought out his violin bow the audience began to get into the spirit of things, and John Bonham's drum solo helped break the ice. An unexpected highlight was John Paul Jones' organ solo on 'Since I've Been Loving You', which provided another preview of the new album. At least it was a highlight for those who could hear the PA system – at the back of the long meadow it might have been another story.

Plant, Page and Jones strummed their gentle acoustic interlude with panache before embarking on a rapid build-up to the grand finale. As dusk fell they played 'How Many More Times' and 'Communication Breakdown' and the crowd went berserk. By 10pm the band had completely won over the long-haired hippie horde.

The exuberant rock'n'roll medley was impossible to follow. Country Joe and The Fish, the very same who had the misfortune to follow Zeppelin on stage back at the Fillmore West, had the further misfortune to follow them again. This time poor old Country Joe had to raise his desperate 'Fish cheer' in pouring rain, at midnight, to folks running for shelter with 'Communication Breakdown' still ringing in their ears.

Zeppelin regarded Bath as their British breakthrough, when fans at home finally took them to their bosom. Said Plant: "We knew it was going to be a crucial gig. When we looked at each other and heard it was sounding good, we looked down and saw everyone else was grooving too."

It's comical to recall that Led Zeppelin were once damned by US music critics for being too loud. *The Los Angeles Times* reviewed the impending third album by suggesting that only drug users could respond to the band's "crushing volume and ferocious histrionics". Clearly they hadn't bothered to listen to an album that

> **❝ WE SPENT THE EVENINGS AROUND LOG FIRES WITH HOT POKERS BEING PLUNGED INTO CIDER. AS THE NIGHTS WORE ON THE GUITARS CAME OUT AND NUMBERS WERE WRITTEN. IT WASN'T PLANNED AS A WORKING HOLIDAY BUT SOME SONGS DID COME OUT OF IT. ❞**
>
> JIMMY PAGE

was subsequently damned for being too quiet! Yet it was the acoustic set, when Plant, Page and Jones sat down to strum their 12-strings and mandolins, that often caused the most impassioned response among true aficionados. Certainly Led Zeppelin were never crudely deafening. Their music was structured in such a way it rarely stayed at the same level or pitch for more than a few minutes at a time, unlike the continuous barrage of later rock bands.

In July the band went on a tour of German cities including Cologne, Essen, Frankfurt and Berlin, while in August they started their sixth American tour and included two sell-out nights at New York's Madison Square Garden. In August Zeppelin also won most of the top slots in the *Melody Maker*'s annual readers' poll, replacing the Beatles as rock's most popular band.

On October 5, 1970 in the US and on October 21 in the UK *Led Zeppelin III* was released with advanced orders of 700,000 copies already racked up in America. Although reviews were mixed, and some fans and critics were put off by the high content of acoustic material, it was a fine album, packed with imaginative performances and with its fair share of new Zeppelin classics.

There was undoubtedly a change in the overall mood and tone, but that was only to be expected from a band determined not to stand still. Encouragingly the album instantly went Gold although it didn't sell quite as well as the first two blockbusters. It was a curious situation: while the band's world-wide audience was expanding at a tremendous rate, Zeppelin fans were listening to, and still discovering, music conceived and largely recorded a year or more earlier. *Led Zeppelin III* reflected a move into new territory, and as usual, the band were ahead of the field.

Perhaps a little too far ahead, because *Led Zeppelin III* was not greeted with critical acclaim. As Page puts it: "The album got a real hammering from the press and I really got brought down by it. I thought the album was good, but we were getting all these knocks and I became very dispirited."

It was probably the skiffle flavour to tunes like 'Bron-Y-Aur Stomp' and the surreal 'Hats Off To (Roy) Harper' that caused most concern to those thirsting for a new 'Communication Breakdown'. There might have been consternation, too, among the record company executives back in New York on hearing the folksy nature of much of the material. But for those with open minds and willing ears, there was much to enjoy and appreciate. Even Zeppelin's most off-the-wall acoustic numbers had a drive no folk band could attain. At the time Robert Plant thought it was the best work the band had done, and, in a sense, the critical backlash was a good thing: it served to spur the band on to even greater efforts.

The *Led Zeppelin III* cover boasted a clever physical design, with a built-in revolving cardboard wheel. Turning the Zeppelin wheel revealed the faces of band members in some eleven holes in the outer cover, surrounded by a collage of surreal images including airships and butterflies. The difficulties in creating this design caused endless delays, and Page was never entirely satisfied with the end result.

New listeners were given a hint of the source of the new material with a brief acknowledgment on the inner gatefold sleeve which read: "Credit must be given to Bron-yr-Aur, a small derelict cottage in South Snowdonia, for painting a somewhat forgotten picture of true completeness which acted as an incentive to some of the musical statements."

However there were somewhat more secretive messages to be found on the record. The original 1970 vinyl copy of the album has the licentious instruction: "Do what thou wilt" unevenly scratched in the stop grooves on side one. Side two has the words "So mote it be" inscribed in the same shaky hand. Putting strange messages like "Porky" on albums was a practice begun by the Beatles, and was usually done as a gag by the chap in charge of pressing the masters. In this case the messenger was Page quoting the instructions of his favourite author and magician, Aleister Crowley, The Great Beast. It seems he rather hoped nobody would spot his handiwork, but eagle-eyed fans rang the record company to ask what it all meant.

Crowley (1875-1947) was a man who had caused great scandal in British society in the 30s; 40 years later he was the subject of many books available in public libraries. Among them was his own work *The Confessions Of Aleister Crowley* (1929). Page was not only interested in Crowley's work but also became a great collector of Crowley's writings and espoused his concepts of sexual magic. He talked enthusiastically about Crowley to anyone who asked, to the point that

Page's interest became the cause of wild rumours and speculation that he was heavily into the occult. However, as 'occult' simply means 'hidden' it didn't necessarily imply any great involvement with nefarious activities.

As Robert Plant has observed since: "He was interested in Crowley as a great British eccentric. He was a very clever man and Page had an innocent interest in him."

Much of Page's interest in Crowley may well have derived from his purchase of Crowley's former home, Boleskin House, situated near to Scotland's Loch Ness. Several unpleasant events had taken place on the site of the house long before Crowley occupied it. At one time a church on the site burned down with members of the congregation inside it.

There was little evidence of dark or Crowlean influences on *Led Zeppelin III*. A more prosaic explanation for the album's sources and intentions was given by Page: "Our albums were mostly a statement of where we were

Aleister Crowley, writer, 'magician' and influence

at the time of recording. But after the second album, which had a lot of hard-hitting rock, the third album was interpreted as us mellowing and losing all our power. The album was to get across more versatility and to use more combinations of instruments. We never stopped doing the heavy things, but there was another side to us."

Some thought it a brave move to forego another bout of screaming and riffing in favour of melody and deeper substance. But Zeppelin simply thought it was the greatest common sense – to go forwards – not backwards.

IMMIGRANT SONG

I was fortunate enough to be in the studio when 'Immigrant Song' was being recorded, and witnessed Page and Bonham laying down the backing tracks one summer's day at Olympic Studios, Barnes. I have

this abiding memory of Page slouching around the small, low-ceilinged room clutching his guitar, and Bonham crouched over his kit, hammering with an intensity that would brook no interruption for small talk or chit chat. Once he got behind the drums, he was gone into another world where he concentrated on generating the heat and the beat to match the sizzling guitar riffs. Page was relaxed and casual as he set up his amp and adjusted the various settings.

I remember noticing how Page and his drummer seemed to be working out the main figure in tandem and how important was Bonham's contribution to shaping the final riff. It turned out to be one of the most powerful in the Zeppelin canon.

The declaiming lyrics reflected Plant's continuing interest in things Celtic and mystical, not to mention those marauding Vikings, and had nothing to do with the philosophies of right-wing politician Enoch Powell. Although the backing tracks were recorded earlier in the year, it was the June trip to Iceland that unleashed Plant's interest in "the land of the ice and snow". The piece begins with an attention-grabbing hiss, which

stemmed from an echo unit feeding back. "Ah - ah!" yells Plant. "We drive our ships to new lands – Valhalla I am coming!" The shimmering guitar creates a surfing accompaniment that summons – for a brief instant – images of Dick Dale of Pulp Fiction fame, before it all comes to an abrupt stop and the Vikings crash out into the sea from whence they came.

Released as a single backed with 'Hey Hey What Can I Do,' in November, 1970, it got to No. 16 during a 13-week run in the US Billboard chart.

FRIENDS

fter some mysterious studio conversations, which seemed to include the use of a familiar four-letter word, the players got down to business, bent on creating an intriguing *pot pourri*. Fierce strumming on the acoustic guitar, over a conga drum rhythm, introduces doomy overtones of Gustav Holst's 'Mars' from *The Planets Suite* – a particular Page favourite. It is also interspersed with a touch of Eastern delight and with the use of a droning synthesizer and deep-toned strings. John Paul Jones is clearly responsible for much of this string-laden background. Slashing guitar chords threaten to slice Page's fingers as he bites into the strings, while Plant mumbles and improvizes his way into the murk. 'Friends' was also recorded as an exercise by Plant and Page with the Bombay Symphony Orchestra on a trip to India, but this is a different full-band version.

CELEBRATION DAY

he synthesizer is still grumbling as Zeppelin take off onto something completely different. Somewhat overlooked and misunderstood at the time, this is just one of the band's less famous items, which have since become strangely relevant and contemporary.

It might be stretching a point to compare this to the latterday works of Black Grape but there is a modern, Manchester sound about this 1970 gem from the archives. The simple, rough-hewn back beat, the clouds of jangling riffs, the hypnotic, trance-like mood. It's a rave all right. This advanced piece of atypical Zeppelin very nearly didn't see the light of day; part of the master tape was crinkled and it wouldn't go through the tape heads. The use of the Moog synthesizer left over from 'Friends' helped disguise the edit required to salvage the track. 'Celebration Day' was played quite frequently on Zeppelin tours, mainly during 1971 and 1972, when the band visited Japan, Britain and Australia.

SINCE I'VE BEEN LOVING YOU

n amazing introduction sets the mood for a piece which stands head and shoulders above everything else on the album. This is not merely one of Led Zeppelin's greatest performances on record, but is a landmark in rock recording.

There is a kind of majestic quality about this soulful display that transcends all the riffing and stomping in the world. It's very moving on several levels. Page plays some of his most heartfelt solo work – not just as a member of a successful rock band turning in another track to complete a scheduled album, but as a creative musician, fulfilling a kind of destiny that is almost unique in the vast outpouring of rock music.

In jazz there are many great and poignant moments: Charlie Parker's 'Lover Man', Duke Ellington's 'Mood Indigo' and Chet Baker's 'My Funny Valentine' spring to mind. Rock tends to be one vast lava flow of amorphous black vinyl untainted by genius, but 'Since I've Been Loving You' stands out. It is something real and complete. So real in fact, that you can hear that faint squeak of Bonham's oil-free bass drum pedal. But as John Paul's organ soothes away the tension, the drums

Producer Page on the alert for crinkled master tape

begin to swing until Bonham sounds like he's sitting in with the full Count Basie orchestra – instead of a four-piece rock group. Even after all these years, it brings a lump to the throat to think of the loss of the man who's drumming is so crucial to this piece's success.

"Working from seven – to eleven" murmurs Plant, beginning a performance that eventually shows the full range of his astounding vocal abilities. There are moments when he sounds not unlike Nina Simone and there are touches of Screaming Jay Hawkins too. But the expression and verbal gymnastics are all Plant's. Page's main solo is full of unremitting power and the ideas flow as he heads towards an inspired but logical conclusion. Great crashing cymbals help to peg the piece in place, while Plant seems to be standing on tiptoe to hit those chattering high notes.

Some have claimed Moby Grape's 'Never' as the inspiration for the tune and certainly the band were one of Plant's favourites. This performance was done virtually live in the studio, with John Paul Jones playing the bass pedals of the Hammond organ with his feet. The blues mood seems almost at odds with the rest of the album's folksy material, and that's because it was originally intended to be included on the more raunchy *Led Zeppelin II* but was held over in favour of 'Whole Lotta Love'.

OUT ON THE TILES

P hil Carson, MD at Atlantic Records in London during the 70s, remembers that John Bonham was the inspiration behind this exuberant performance. "He used to have a little ditty that he would sing when we were going out to play. The song went: 'I've had a pint of bitter and now I'm feeling better and I'm out on the tiles. We're going down the rubbers and we're going to pull some scrubbers because we're out on the tiles,' " he recalls.

"Bonham made that song up. Rubbers refers to 'rub-a-dub-dubs' – clubs of course. Page turned the tune that John sang into a riff, and that's the derivation of 'Out On The Tiles'. It was probably the most fun song Zeppelin ever did!"

Bonham's lyrics however were replaced by something more suitable for general consumption, although Plant retains the jaunty air of a reprobate on the prowl. "As I walk down the highway all I do is sing this song," he says, addressing a band frantically engaged in bashing out a singularly violent riff. A rumbling, grumbling guitar is locked in deadly embrace with the drums, which trip over themselves into a brace of accents that sound like a warning cry of "Uh oh, uh oh!" Whichever club they are heading for, there is obviously bound to be trouble before the night is out. When Plant sings "I'm so glad I'm leaving you" a ghostly voice can be detected in the mix pleading "stay".

Trouble brewing. Bonham gears up for a night on the tiles

GALLOWS POLE

A traditional folk tune, based on a work by Huddie Ledbetter (known as Leadbelly) the celebrated American blues singer, prison convict, 12-string guitarist, and folk composer. Leadbelly's version of the song was called 'Gallis Pole' and it has also been called 'Maid Freed From The Gallows' and 'Gallows Line'.

In this version Page plays banjo, 6-string and 12-string guitars as well as lead electric. John Paul Jones adds the mandolin. It was one of the first times Page had ever played the banjo, which he borrowed from Jones. He'd first heard the song played on a record by 12-string-guitar-player Fred Gerlach, and devised this arrangement for the band who performed it in Copenhagen on their 1971 European tour.

Plant pleads with the hangman to wait a while as he sees first his friends, then his brother and sister coming to the rescue, bearing gifts of silver and gold. Will his execution be stayed, or will he soon be swinging from the gallows pole? As the singer becomes increasingly desperate, drums and banjo launch into an incongruously jolly rhythm that creates a kind of danse macabre.

A strangely exciting climax is reached in which tradition is turned on its head and a full-blooded Zeppelin *tour de force* takes over. This was one of Page's personal favourites from the album, and from time to time Plant made references to the song by tossing a few lines from 'Gallows Pole' into other tunes like 'Trampled Underfoot' from *Physical Graffiti*.

**Opposite:
Beards and moustaches
were all the rage in 1970**

**Leadbelly, American
folk/blues legend
and composer of
'Gallows Pole'**

Finger pickin' god

TANGERINE

After a false start, Page sets off on acoustic guitar to deliver a very pretty ballad that had its origins in a tune previously written and recorded by him with the Yardbirds. Page delays his entrance in order to set the right tempo. He plays pedal steel guitar, creating the kind of country ballad that you'd expect to hear on the radio while driving a pick-up truck across the Texas plains.

Plant intones Page's words with tender care. "Think how it used to be," he murmurs, on a song of lost love and a fondly remembered past affair. Although quite sweet and brief, the piece doesn't stop changing tack for more than a few bars at a time, revealing the arranger's craft and skill at sustaining interest. No drum machines or tape loops here. 'Tangerine' was frequently played on the band's acoustic set until the summer of 1972, and was revived for the Earls Court, London shows of 1975.

THAT'S THE WAY

A singularly attractive and pleasant performance that, above all, shows the difference between perceived ideas about the band's musical aims and ambitions and Zeppelin's own philosophy. Here are fine melodies and lofty sentiments, far removed from the grosser aspects of Zeppelin output. The acoustic guitars swirl and cosset a theme rich in images of velvet clothes, burning incense, golden hair and mountain streams. A love song steeped in poetry in which brutish drums and metallic guitars are banished. Only a gently jingling tambourine keeps up a steady rhythm, while Plant sings "Yesterday I saw you standing by the river" – one of those intimacies guaranteed to clutch at a young girl's heart. And then he adds: "Yesterday I saw you kiss tiny flowers."

At this point one might have expected Bonham to start demolishing the studio furniture with scornful fury, but he keeps a respectful distance and joins in the folk club spirit. Originally titled 'The Boy Next Door' (one of the lines), it is clearly a product of the writing sessions at Bron-yr-Aur cottage and reflects Plant's desire to escape from the harsh realities of life on the road into a more romantic world of peace and love.

As he later explained: "The great thing about our stay in Snowdonia was there was no motion, just privacy and nature and the beauty of the people there. It was a good experience in every way." During the trip Page and Plant often went for walks around the countryside armed with a tape recorder to make sure that if a good idea came up it wouldn't go to waste. 'That's The Way' came about in this fashion. Page told me: "This was written in Wales when Robert and I stayed at the cottage. It was one of those days after a long walk and we were setting back . . . we had a guitar with us. It was a tiring walk coming down a ravine, so we stopped and sat down. I played the tune and Robert sang a verse straight off. We had the tape recorder ready and got the tune down."

BRON-Y-AUR STOMP

This particular ditty was written in honour of Plant's pet dog Strider and not, as one might suspect, in honour of one of his early girlfriends. Strider, incidentally, was named after Aragorn's alter-ego in JRR Tolkien's *Lord Of The Rings*. As Page launches into some nimble finger-pickin', bluegrass style, Plant tells how he walks down a country lane – "Calling your name".

This canine boogie is enlivened by Bonham playing spoons and castanets. John Paul Jones uses an acoustic five-string fretless bass to get an authentic Lonnie-Donegan-style skiffle feel. The tune has its origins in a piece called 'Jennings Farm Blues', which the band played at the beginning of these *Led Zeppelin III* sessions. The 'Stomp' was recorded at Headley Grange in 1970, using the Stones' mobile, and finished off at Island, London and Ardent Studios, Memphis, Tennessee. It was played live during Zeppelin's 1972 tours of the UK, US and Japan and at Earls Court in 1975.

HATS OFF TO (ROY) HARPER

Jimmy Page had met the great Liverpool-born folk singer at the Bath Festival and he was an uncompromising, charismatic artist whom both Plant and Page admired. This song was intended as a tribute to Harper, who never managed to attain major success or recognition.

Harper became a friend of the band and went on tour with them as an opening act. He also enjoyed the lifestyle and the perks of being behind the scenes with the Zeppelin entourage, which proved to be quite an eye-opener. In later years, Page and Harper would record an album together called *Whatever Happened To Jugula* (1985).

'Hats Off' achieves a remarkably authentic traditional sound and is based on a Bukka White blues called 'Shake Em On Down'. It features some of Jimmy Page's finest bottleneck guitar work. Plant sings with all the primitive intensity of a 1920s country bluesman, and you can almost imagine him pulling on a jug of whiskey, while waiting for the train whistle to blow, the levée to break and the sun to go down.

Supposedly composed by one 'Charles Obscure' and never performed live, 'Hats Off' was greeted with some dismay by hardcore Zeppelin fans on first hearing. It seemed a low-key way to end such a crucial album. However the piece has grown in stature over the years, and curiously enough now seems as authentically ancient as the original blues 78 rpm records did, when viewed from the 70s.

Roy Harper (with hat off)

4 FOUR SYMBOLS

(ATLANTIC K 50002 RE-ISSUE NO.25008) 1971

Untitled, Four Symbols – it really didn't matter what it was called. From the riff laden 'Black Dog' to the triumphal 'Stairway To Heaven' and cataclysmic 'When The Levee Breaks' this was their finest hour.

BLACK DOG

ROCK AND ROLL

THE BATTLE OF EVERMORE

STAIRWAY TO HEAVEN

MISTY MOUNTAIN HOP

FOUR STICKS

GOING TO CALIFORNIA

WHEN THE LEVEE BREAKS

ne of the most fruitful and consistent of all Zeppelin albums, *Four Symbols* was greeted with less hysteria on initial release than earlier blockbusters. This may have been because the world had grown to expect an annual Led Zeppelin release, or had given up trying to guess which way the band would turn next. Yet the new album proved that after the mild disappointments of their previous effort, Zeppelin were in cracking form and consolidating their dual-pronged acoustic/heavy rock approach. They may have taken the less favourable reviews and reaction to *Led Zeppelin III* on board and mapped out a more vibrant, cohesive plan of attack. Said Jimmy Page: "We thought we'd done a really good album. We knew there was good material on it. Yet it got slammed because they said we'd started to play acoustic instruments, just because

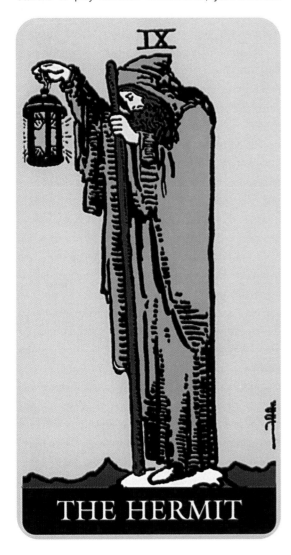

THE HERMIT

Crosby, Stills and Nash had just come out." Released in November 1971, the new album was packed with performances that would become classics and ensure that the band became enshrined in legend. 'Stairway To Heaven' shone like a beacon, becoming not only their most famous song, but also one of rock's greatest anthems. In a curious way, it didn't instantly grab the attention of record buyers. It was not as obvious as bravura performances like 'Black Dog' and 'Rock And Roll'. However, the subtle qualities of the song, its sophisticated arrangement and its poignant lyrics, gained greater appreciation over the days and years, rather like a fine wine maturing and increasing in value and appeal. Just as Eric Clapton found 'Layla' a slow-burning fuse, so Led Zeppelin discovered that their big ballad, introduced to live shows earlier in the year, ignited a fizz and crackle of excitement that eventually spread around the world. Audiences raised their blazing cigarette lighters in supplication every time Page's opening notes rent the air at festivals and concerts. Just as 'Stairway' increased in stature, so the rest of the *Four Symbols* songs like 'Misty Mountain Hop', 'The Battle Of Evermore' and 'Four Sticks' gained a reputation that helped put the album firmly in the hall of fame.

The band started work at Island Studios, a converted church in London, during December 1970, but after Christmas moved back to the somewhat tumbled-down mansion at Headley Grange, Hampshire, where they had worked before. They brought in the Rolling Stones' mobile studio truck, along with Ian 'Stu' Stewart, a Stones employee and part-time piano player who jammed on 'Rock And Roll'. Part of the reason the house was ramshackle was that the band had burnt some of the banisters to keep warm on their previous visit. The fire was lit again during this latest visit, which led some to fear that the entire building might eventually be sacrificed to the flames. It was in front of the log fire that Robert Plant eventually wrote part of the lyrics to 'Stairway To Heaven'. Jimmy Page was particularly fond of the three-storey building, which provided both facilities and atmosphere. Explained Page: "We often rehearsed at Headley Grange, and we were used to the place. It was familiar territory. We even lived there during rehearsals. I think Fleetwood Mac first suggested we use the place. They had rehearsed there at some time and we decided to go in

The Hermit from The Tarot, as depicted on the original album sleeve

there with a recording truck. That was the beginning of the Headley period. There was some stuff on the following albums like *Houses Of The Holy* and *Physical Graffiti* that was done there as well."

Not all of the band liked the Grange – it had once been a Victorian workhouse and both Plant and Bonham were a little spooked by it. Furthermore, engineer Andy Johns was convinced the house was haunted. The next time the band visited the place, all except Page retired to stay at a nearby hotel. But Headley Grange was noted for its amazing acoustics, and these helped provide a particularly powerful drum sound, which was put to good use on Zeppelin's most atmospheric piece, the much discussed 'When The Levee Breaks'. Said Page: "There was an open hallway with a staircase going up, and that's where we got that drum sound. It was a pretty austere place but I loved the atmosphere." Apart from the sound, there was also the convenience of living over the shop. As soon as the band dreamt up an idea, they could put it down on tape without having to wait to book time at a regular studio. However, this process did have its pitfalls, as Page recalls: "In a way, it was a good method. The only thing wrong was that we'd get so excited about an idea that we'd really rush to finish its format to get it on tape." Among the songs written at the Grange were 'Misty Mountain Hop' and 'The Battle Of Evermore'. The album was eventually finished in February, 1971.

When the album was due for release, Page decided to leave it untitled, rather than call it *Led Zeppelin IV*. Peter Grant, their manager, also thought they should leave the name off, especially when a plan to feature each member of the band on the sleeve came to nothing – nobody could agree whose picture should be on the front. Record executives were alarmed when they heard of the plan, assuring Page he would be committing 'professional suicide' by leaving the name

> **"THERE WAS AN OPEN HALLWAY WITH A STAIRCASE GOING UP, AND THAT'S WHERE WE GOT THAT DRUM SOUND. IT WAS A PRETTY AUSTERE PLACE BUT I LOVED THE ATMOSPHERE."**
>
> JIMMY PAGE

of the band off the sleeve. "I had to talk like hell to get that done," he admitted later. Indeed, there was no text at all on the cover, only a picture of an old countryman wearing a kind of shovel hat, and sporting a whiskery beard. This curious figure was bent double under the weight of a bundle of rods. His image was set in a battered picture frame, hung on a partially demolished wall, covered in peeling floral wall paper. When the sleeve was folded out, it became clear that the wall was part of a house being demolished on a slum clearance site. An unreadable Oxfam poster, on the wall of one of the remaining buildings, contained the only words on the sleeve. Taken as a whole, the design was a bold step and curiously effective.

The inner sleeve showed a charcoal drawing by Page's friend Barrington Colby. This depicted a hooded hermit holding a lantern illuminated by a star, standing on a mountainous pile of rocks, overlooking a distant walled city. It is said that he represents *The Hermit*, Number IX of the tarot cards, usually portrayed as a bearded monk holding a lamp to light the way. The Hermit looks back on his past and realizes that there is more to life than he knows. The card stands for caution, patience, prudence and wisdom. Said Page: "The idea represents the ascension to the beacon and the light of truth." He also felt it reflected an attitude of mind and a philosophy that combined the twin ideals of hard work and aspiration.

While salesmen looked askance at this anonymous album, there was little danger that rock fans would miss the latest Zeppelin release, and the band did plenty of interviews. But it was a strange looking bunch that the press met – the pressures of fame had caused Zeppelin to retreat from their perceived glam rock image especially while walking on the streets. On stage during the early 70s, Jimmy Page epitomized the slim and beautiful, aesthetic youth, with his mass of black curly hair and bejewelled, embroidered outfits. Now he and his mates adopted straggly beards and dressed like electric gypsies. It reflected their genuine desire for people to judge their efforts on merit alone. According to Page: "We decided that on the fourth album we would deliberately play down the group name and there wouldn't be any information whatsoever on the outer jacket. Names don't mean a thing. What does 'Led Zeppelin' mean? What matters is our music." Page repeatedly tried to explain the significance of the cover design: "The old man on the cover carrying the wood is in harmony with nature. He takes from nature and gives back to the land. It's a natural circle. It's right. His old cottage gets pulled down and they put him in slums, terrible places." This was one version. Some assiduous students of the occult later carefully studied the picture and claimed to identify the old man under the bundle of rods as a 19th century English magician who rejoiced under the name of George Pickingale. His knowledge was later passed on to Aleister Crowley, with whom Page was so fascinated. A more prosaic explanation for the mystery was that the picture of the old man was simply something that Plant found in a shop in Reading. Page remembers: "Robert and I came up with the design together. Robert bought the print that is on the cover from a junk shop!"

Certainly the untitled album caused problems for chart compilers, as well as nervous record bosses. "Basically the whole title thing was just another ruse to throw the media into chaos, and we all had a good laugh when the record went into the charts and they had to reproduce the symbols instead of a title!" related Page. Led Zeppelin's 1971 epic was eventually listed either as *Untitled* or *Four Symbols*, after the runic symbols that appeared on the centre label. When I met John Bonham in a bar in London's Charing Cross Road that autumn to discuss the new album, he drew the four symbols in my note book and asked me to guess which member of the band they represented. It wasn't too difficult – Robert Plant was the feather, while the three strong intertwined rings belonged to John Bonham. Zoso was Jimmy Page's magical symbol and a mesh of elliptical shapes represented John Paul Jones. Bonham explained: "The cover means whatever people want to read into it. For me it means: 'I'd rather live in an old house than a block of flats.' My personal view is that the album is the best thing we've ever done. I love it. All the albums have been different and to my mind this is the best – and that's not trying to be big-headed or flash. The playing is some of the best we have ever done. The runes are symbols that simply apply to each of us."

Bonham always preferred a down-to-earth explanation to the magical side of Zeppelin and, in any case, Page didn't discuss his studies into the occult with anybody, especially not fellow members of the band. However, it is always fun to investigate, and close scrutiny of the famous symbols on a spinning LP disk showed they had a strange life of their own, jiggling in an unearthly fashion before the eyes. Embedded in the black vinyl of side one of the original pressings are the words "Pecko Duck"; on side two appears the single inscription "Porky". While some scholars thought these sayings might have some bizarre sexual connotation or occult significance, a substantial body of opinion has now come to the conclusion that "Porky" is merely the nickname of the man who cut the masters, one George Peckham of Porky's Disc Cutting Service.

Robert Plant explained that each member of the band chose his own metaphysical symbol to depict his personality. "It would represent a state of mind, an opinion, or something we felt strongly about" he said. Plant's own feather symbol was supposedly drawn from sacred symbols of the ancient Mu civilisation of some 15,000 years ago, whose inhabitants lived on a lost continent now believed to be situated under the Pacific Ocean. However, Page has said it was just something Plant drew himself. "The feather is a symbol on which all sorts of philosophies have been based and which has a very interesting heritage. It represented courage to the Red Indian tribes."

John Paul Jones' symbol was one of two found in a tome called *The Book Of Signs*, compiled by Rudolf Koch. Jones' sign represents "a confident and competent personality", supposedly because it is difficult to draw accurately. Interestingly, this sign is also said to exorcize evil spirits. John Bonham's sign came from the same book and was one he identified with on sight. The three rings represent The Trinity, while the inner shield depicts strength and unity. Robert Plant noted that it was also the symbol of a brand of American beer.

As for Page's own symbol, Zozo which he used to decorate the pair of tight black velvet pants he wore on stage, it is a design rather than a pronounceable word. Astrologers have deduced that the symbol is made up

> **" NAMES DON'T MEAN A THING. WHAT DOES 'LED ZEPPELIN' MEAN? WHAT MATTERS IS OUR MUSIC. "**
>
> JIMMY PAGE

of various parts, including Hebraic runes which indicate Page's own star signs, split between solar Capricorn and lunar Cancer, with Scorpio rising. It reveals him as a secretive person who is eager to find knowledge, truth and inner wisdom. Says Page: "My symbol is one which I designed myself, but a lot of people mistake it for a word 'Zoso' and some people in the States still refer to the record as 'Zoso'. This is a pity, because it wasn't supposed to be a word at all, but something entirely different and with a different meaning altogether." When I talked to Jim about the album shortly after its release, he was more keen to discuss the music than the symbols.

"We know where we're going as a group. We're four individuals who have found a common denominator in music. There is a lot of inspiration coming through on this album. We're getting better all the time. There is quite a lot of instrumental work on the record. On our gigs we try to cut down the volume. There are so many complaints about volume and people liken us to Grand Funk Railroad. I can't see any comparison. We did acoustic things on our first album and I would have thought that created a precedent for us."

Led Zeppelin IV, *Four Symbols*, *Untitled* – call it what you will. This was a band still setting precedents.

The basic recordings for the album were completed during February 1971. There was trouble with the mixing in Los Angeles and much of the material had to be re-done, which delayed the release of the album until the end of the year. These problems also scuppered tentative plans to make the new one a double album. It was engineer Andy Johns' idea to mix the album at Sunset Sound, LA; he found on his arrival that the studio he'd used before had changed. He found another room, mixed the album and brought it back to London to play to the group. In his own words: "It sounded awful." In the end, the whole album had to be remixed at Island Studios back in London. Jimmy Page was not best pleased and pointed out that they

> **"WE KNOW WHERE WE'RE GOING AS A GROUP. WE'RE FOUR INDIVIDUALS WHO HAVE FOUND A COMMON DENOMINATOR IN MUSIC."**
>
> JIMMY PAGE

could easily have gone to the nearest studio to mix the album, rather than trek all the way to California just for the sunshine.

In March the band began a series of British tour dates, which included an exciting trip to Ireland where they showcased their latest material. It was during their Belfast gig that they first unleashed 'Stairway To Heaven' to wild acclaim. They played their thank you dates to British fans on their 'Back To The Small Clubs' tour, which was supposed to bring back the flavour of the old days. However, when this meant cramped dressing rooms, lousy back stage food and tiny venues that didn't earn money, it was realized that the good old days weren't quite so good after all. From then on it was back to the stadiums, and room service. During July they went to Europe for a tour, and suffered horrendous riots in a football stadium in Milan when the Italian police attacked fans with tear gas. The band had to flee the stage and their road crew were stretchered out after trying to save the equipment, amid clouds of gas. John Paul Jones later described the scene as "a war zone". In August the band returned to the relative safety of America and embarked on their seventh US tour, playing 20 concerts which grossed over a million dollars. After a short holiday, the band went to Japan for five shows, including a charity show for the victims of the atom bomb at Hiroshima. In November, 1971, the album went to No.1 in the UK and No.2 in the US charts. The band went on a major UK tour and played two dates at Wembley Arena in London, which sold out overnight. The following month, 'Black Dog' was released as a single in the States and spent 11 weeks in the charts. The band were still fighting the idea of releasing singles, but the pressure on them to give way was enormous.

It is strange to think that just a few months prior to all the activity that surrounded the release of *Four Symbols*, the rock world had been swept by rumours that the band might break up. As John Bonham said: "I hate it when people slag us off. We had done three tours during 1970 and we finished off feeling we had just about had enough. We had done so much in such a short space of time, we were drained. We had offers to go everywhere and we could have done them. But what would have been the point? We were tired. We had worked hard and needed a break before we got stale. We spent six months at home and writing songs, then we said 'Right, let's go.' We didn't do any gigs but there was absolutely no intention of splitting up. We had so many great ideas to use on the new album. John Paul Jones was incredible, coming to the studio each day with new instruments to play."

Back in November 1971, John Bonham tried to answer speculation about the future music of Led Zeppelin. "Bloody hard to say. I can't say what we are going to sound like in the future and I don't really want to know. If I could tell you what we're going to sound like in two years time, it would ruin it anyway. We might be on top next year, or I might be back on the buildings!"

BLACK DOG

Black Dog' was one of the heaviest Zeppelin riffs of all time, and one that was beloved of the new breed of heavy rock bands who emerged a decade later. Many wondered if the name was inspired by some strange mythical beast, but there is a more prosaic explanation for this particular apparition: it was named after a friendly mutt seen lurching about the building during the sessions.

A distant guitar warms up, giving some idea of the strange ambience at Headley Grange. Andy Johns says the band recorded the basic track for this one in what had once been a crypt. Robert Plant's voice, bold, sensuous and oozing sweat and sex, yells to the rooftops: "Hey, hey Mama, said the way you move, gonna make you sweat, gonna make you groove!" Here Led Zeppelin display their complete grasp of the use of dynamics. The entire band answer Plant's lone exclamations in unison. There's no danger of missing a syllable of his vocal statements, as the "call and response" blues routine underpins his vocal attack. This ruse was inspired in part by Fleetwood Mac's 'Oh Well' but it was also a device frequently used in traditional jazz and blues. An unexpected Latin funk groove from Bonham lifts the piece out of the rhythmic rut, while Page's guitar riff is astonishingly basic but entirely self-assured. In fact the piece chugs over an odd time signature (a mixture of 4/4 set against 5/4) and is full of unpredictable rests, which belie its apparent simplicity. John Paul Jones was responsible for the riff and

arrangement, while Page overdubbed no less than four guitar tracks using a Gibson Les Paul guitar put through a direct injection box. Andy Johns recalls that they tripled-tracked three rhythm guitars to get a satisfying stereo spread. Page later said that the band always tried to encourage the laid back John Paul Jones to write more material, and this was undoubtedly one of his most effective and powerful themes. The strange noise at the beginning of the piece was, as Page described it: "The guitar army waking up. Rise and shine!"

> **❝ I CAN'T SAY WHAT WE ARE GOING TO SOUND LIKE IN THE FUTURE AND I DON'T REALLY WANT TO KNOW. ❞**
>
> JOHN BONHAM

"You want heavy? You got heavy"

Among cover versions of the song are one by the band Let's Active, while Dread Zeppelin mixed up the tune with 'Hound Dog', resulting in a line that went "You ain't nuthin' but a black dog." Robert Plant also sampled part of the tune for 'Tall Cool One' from his 'Now And Zen' solo album.

'Black Dog' remained a favourite on live shows until it was replaced by material from 'Presence' during their 1977 US tour. It was released as a single in the US in December 1971, and got to No.15 in the Billboard chart. Peter Grant used to rage and fulminate against his American record company executives when they insisted on releasing singles against his wishes. In fact he only achieved the co-operation of Phil Carson, who was Atlantic's chief in London on this matter, which was why the 'no singles' policy only really worked in the UK. As Grant constantly explained, Zeppelin tracks would need editing if they were to be released in this fashion, thus spoiling the musical content, and in any case the albums would sell even more copies if they contained the tracks people most wanted to hear.

ROCK AND ROLL

Rock and roll' – Led Zeppelin let their hair down on this celebration of the golden age of innocence. This was the way countless British beat groups interpreted American rock of the 50s, when Page, Plant, Bonham and Jones were teenagers. It was a nostalgic trip in 1971, and still retains its authentic flavour in the 90s. In fact 'Rock And Roll' has become something of a standard for today's bar bands and support groups. The crashing hi-hat and snare drum introduction that sets the mood has been assiduously copied by sweating drummers around the world, hoping to get it right, while every lead singer has to practise Plant's famously drawn out "Lonely, lonely, lonely time!' The band get the high-stepping beat just right – not too fast or slow – while a boogie piano in the background (courtesy of Ian Stewart) adds a suitable barrage of 'plink, plink, plinks' behind Plant's increasingly hysterical vocals. "Oh yeah!" is just about as deep as he gets on this one, but with a suitably crazed guitar solo to top off the madness, this is Zeppelin having fun.

According to Page, the drum intro was inspired by the original recording of Little Richard's 'Keep A-Knockin', which Bonham began playing one afternoon while the tape was still running. They were supposed to be recording another piece, but Bonham's impatience signalled the need for something to break the tension. Page got stuck into a suitable riff which he later confessed "ground to a halt after 12 bars."

But Plant began improvising a vocal and soon the throwaway piece was fashioned into a new Zeppelin standard. Says Page: "It was spontaneous combustion. I think we might have been attempting 'Four Sticks' and it wasn't actually happening that day." Bonham just started drumming and, says Page: "I played a riff automatically and that was 'Rock And Roll'. I think we got through the whole of the first 12 bars and said, 'Wait a minute, this is great. Forget 'Four Sticks', let's work on this.' That's one we literally did on the spot. I think we did it in three or four takes."

The number was incorporated into the band's touring set and it became a regular encore from 1971 until it was redeployed as an opening number, then put into a medley with 'Whole Lotta Love'. 'Rock And Roll' has been played regularly whenever ex-Zeppelin men get together, notably at Live Aid and Jason Bonham's wedding. It's also been played regularly by such bands as Def Leppard and Heart, while John Bonham's sister Debbie sings the number with her own band.

"Rock And Roll chaps!"

Sandy Denny, of Fairport Convention, duetted with Plant on 'The Battle Of Evermore'. Sandy died in 1978 from injuries caused by a fall

THE BATTLE OF EVERMORE

The late Sandy Denny, of Fairport Convention, was called in to share vocal duties with Plant on this attractive, moody acoustic piece, inspired by tales of the Scottish wars. The melody was created by Jimmy Page while playing John Paul Jones' mandolin one evening at the manor house, after the rest of the band had retired for the evening. He began experimenting with chords and a new number began to emerge from his tentative strumming. Said Page: "It may have sounded like a dance-around-the-maypole number, but it wasn't purposely like that. I used Jonesy's mandolin on that. We were living in the house and some would go to bed early and I used to sit up and play quite a bit. I picked up the mandolin and this tune just came out. I'd never played one before, and the tuning's totally different, but there was something about that period. It was a time of great inspiration."

Plant had read a book about Scottish history before

going to Headley Grange and described 'The Battle Of Evermore' as: "More of a playlet than a song. After I wrote the lyrics, I realized I needed another completely different voice to give the song its full impact." Zeppelin had once appeared on stage at the Los Angeles Troubadour club in 1970 with Fairport Convention, the British folk rock group they greatly admired. Fairport were recording a live album there and the Zep men cheerfully joined in, playing under the pseudonym of the Birmingham Water Buffalo Society. Hence the call to Sandy Denny to sing on the track. In the story she was to act as the voice of a town crier, urging the people to throw down their weapons. Denny later said that Plant left her completely exhausted after their session together. As a reward, Denny was given her own special symbol of three pyramids on the album sleeve.

The marriage of rock and folk music had begun on the tour preceding the release of the album, when Zeppelin's acoustic set had been developed in the teeth of yelling fans. "Shut up and listen," was invariably the cry from Plant, followed by a kinder "Give us a kiss!" Unlike the other major acoustic number on the album, 'The Battle Of Evermore' was rarely unleashed live, although it was played during the band's 1977 US tour. Page played mandolin, John Paul Jones played a triple-neck acoustic and also sang the lines originally delivered by Sandy Denny, with somewhat less flair. The song was also covered by The Love Mongers in a 1992 grunge movie called *Singles*.

STAIRWAY TO HEAVEN

Hailed as simply the finest rock ballad of all time, the track slipped almost unnoticed into the general public's consciousness as the band gradually introduced it into their live act. Their fans, of course, hearing it at such venues at the LA Forum, greeted it with tremendous applause. The first British fans heard of the rather good new Zep number was when it was played at a particularly exciting and memorable

gig at Belfast's Ulster Hall, on March 5, 1971.

The band had arrived in Northern Ireland at a time when 'The Troubles' were at their height. In fact violent riots were going on just a few streets away during the concert, as an official later informed the fearful party of press and musicians. A petrol tanker was hijacked, a youth was shot dead and fire bombs were hurled the night Zeppelin came to town. Yet there was no hint of violence or trouble during the show. Quite the reverse. The band were showered with affection by a crowd almost hysterical in their appreciation and enthusiasm. Here was a rock band that actually had the courage to tour during a dangerous time. They kicked off with 'Immigrant Song' and previewed quite a bit of material from the fourth album that evening, including 'Black Dog.'

After a stunning version of 'Dazed And Confused' came the new unheralded song that at first intrigued and then swept away the audience. The magic and pathos of the piece seemed to be even more relevant in the warring atmosphere of the times. During the performance, Page played a double-necked guitar utilising both twelve and six strings. The finger-picked contrapuntal guitar intro became one of rock's best known phrases, beloved of all aspiring guitarists – and actually banned from being played in some musical instrument shops along with Deep Purple's 'Smoke On The Water'. Plant sang the romantic tale with all the passion at his command. If Plant announced it to the crowd, the title could barely be heard above the din.

The set broke up with all the casual disorganisation and lack of security of the times. "That's all, boys and girls, please go home now!" yelled the promoter, standing in the middle of the hall like a slightly distraught youth club organizer. Fans flocked unhindered into the band's tiny dressing room and an Irish Colleen looked at the visitors with some amazement. "They were really fantastic," she told me, "are they an English band? I thought they were from America. I always thought Robert Plant was fat and Jimmy Page was tall, from the picture I have at home. You get these funny notions."

I had a funny notion that the new song would be a hit and Plant was smiling when he talked about it on

> **" I KNEW IT WAS GOING TO BE A MONSTER. I DIDN'T KNOW IT WOULD BECOME A BLOODY ANTHEM! "**
>
> ANDY JOHNS

Overleaf: Feeling a little Zoso Zoso, Page employs his famed double-neck guitar

the flight back to London. It was a wonder that Plant was in a mood to smile – the night before Bonham had aimed a punch at his head during an altercation in the hotel. I quaked in my hotel bedroom as I heard the row blazing and Bonham pounding on Peter Grant's door. "Peter, I've done something terrible. I've hit Robert!" "Shut up. And go to bed," growled Grant from the depths of his room. I never found out what caused the argument, but I had seen Plant earlier offering Bonham a banana after he'd completed his drum solo, as if rewarding a particularly clever chimp. They had a way of winding each other up.

On the flight home, Page, quiet, polite and friendly as ever, told me about the new songs on *Led Zeppelin IV*. He explained that the intro to 'Stairway' on the record also featured wooden recorders played by John Paul Jones. "We can't reproduce them on stage, but the acoustic guitars come off well. The words are brilliant – they are the best Robert has ever written." The song had been assembled through a process of trial and experiment, but came together quite quickly. At the recording session they had put down a rehearsal version on tape first, which helped put the words into focus. Page later said: "I had 'Stairway' tucked away on my cassettes. Robert arrived at Headley Grange quite late in the day and I'd actually got all the musical part together from beginning to end. Robert came in with 60 per cent of the lyrics off the cuff, which was quite something. He was listening to the music, sitting on a stool by a log fire and jotting away, and suddenly he came out with all these lyrics. When we were recording it, there were little bits, little sections that I'd done. I was getting reference pieces down on cassette, and sometimes I referred back to them if I felt there was something right that could be included."

The crucial moment after the acoustic build up, when John Bonham comes in with all drums blazing, was a brilliant touch. As Page remembers: "It was an idea I'd used before, to give it that extra kick. Then there's a fanfare towards the solo and Robert comes in with his tremendous vocal. 'Stairway To Heaven' crystallized the essence of the band. It had everything there and showed the band at its best. We were careful never to release it as a single. It was a milestone for us. Every musician wants to do something of lasting quality, something that will hold up for a long time, and I guess we did it with 'Stairway'."

The bulk of the eight-minute piece, including Page's fiery Fender Telecaster guitar solo over those familiar series of grandiose chords, was recorded at Island Studios in London, rather than at Headley Grange. Page knew it was going to be a complex construction and he needed full studio facilities to complete the production work. One of the most difficult moments came when Bonham had to slot in the right beats when the 12-string section led into the main guitar solo. Engineer Andy Johns remembers that the song and its arrangement were done before the band came into the studio, then it was cut in straightforward fashion with Jimmy Page on acoustic guitar, John Paul Jones at an upright Hohner electric piano and John Bonham sat behind his kit. Once some bass had been put on, Page began adding guitar overdubs. "I knew it was going to be a monster," recalls the engineer. "I didn't know it would become a bloody anthem!"

The full impact of the songs only really sank in when the album was finally released. Over the following years, as the song grew in stature, it became the most played track of all time on US radio. In London it became No.1 in Capital Radio's *Top Five Hundred*, just one of many awards it picked up. As late as 1983 it was voted 'All Time Greatest Track' in the UK *Kerrang!* magazine's reader's poll. In fact the buzz about the song grew to embarrassing proportions, which, in later years, led Plant to disown the blatant romanticism of the tale of the gilded lady. He almost refused to sing it when the band got together for their 1985 Live Aid appearance and dropped it from the Page-Plant tour of 1995, saying it was now irrelevant in a tougher age of rock. He felt there were many other Zeppelin songs that he could relate to with more confidence. He insisted that 'Kashmir' was the definitive Zeppelin song and not 'Stairway', which he called a "a nice, pleasant, well-meaning, naïve, very English little song." Yet Plant created genuine poetry with his selected use of words and imagery and there was no hint of cloying

> **" WAS I UPSET ABOUT ROLF DOING 'STAIRWAY TO HEAVEN'? NO, NOT AT ALL. I'LL GET MY OWN BACK. WHEN I GET BACK ON THE ROAD I'LL DO A COUPLE OF ROLF HARRIS SONGS! "**
>
> ROBERT PLANT

sweetness or banality in his opening line: "There's a lady who's sure all that glitters is gold and she's buying a stairway to heaven." The lyrics were tastefully reproduced on the LPs inner sleeve in special lettering that Page discovered in a back issue of an old arts magazine, *Studio*.

Plant recalls that work on the song began after Bonham and Jones left Headley Grange for the evening to visit London's Speakeasy Club, a popular musicians'

Engulfed in dry ice, Robert Plant climbs the 'Stairway To Heaven'

watering hole. "Jimmy and I stayed and we got the themes and thread of it right there and then. The lyrics were a cynical thing about a woman getting everything she wanted all the time without giving anything back. It was all done very quickly. It was a very fluid, unnaturally easy track. There was something pushing it, saying 'You guys are okay but if you want to do something timeless, here's a wedding song for you.'"

Curiously, a phrase similar to Zeppelin's appears on

'Skip Softly My Moonbeams', a track on the 1968 Procol Harum album *Shine On Brightly*. Gary Brooker sings the Keith Reid lyric which goes: "The stairs to heaven lead straight down to hell." However, Reid does not believe there is any connection with the Led Zeppelin classic. "I've never even been aware of that. I shouldn't think Zeppelin ever noticed it, either. It's just one of those great coincidences," reflects Keith. Even stranger is the fact that Brooklyn-born songwriter Neil Sedaka had a Top 10 hit in America with a song called 'Stairway To Heaven', in 1960, but nobody remembered it during the Zeppelin era a decade later.

For Page it remains a magical piece of work, a flowing melody which he would only play as an instrumental when he returned as a solo artist, after the demise of Zeppelin. No one other than Plant would be allowed to sing it. In 1982, at a charity concert held in London's Royal Albert Hall, he played it with almost demonic energy. With a cigarette pasted on his lower lip, clutching his guitar, he struggled around the stage, as if literally rebuilding his life before the eyes of an appreciative audience.

There was always a huge demand for the song to be released as a single, but the band and their management resisted the idea. Said Page: "They tried everything to convince us it should come out as a single, but we just said 'no'. It would have destroyed the whole feel of the album." As with previous Zep albums containing obvious hits, the LP topped the charts on both sides of the Atlantic. In fact 'Stairway' was briefly issued on a rare picture disc in the US with 'Hey Hey What Can I Do' on the B-side. In Australia an EP appeared called 'The Acoustic Side Of Zeppelin' which featured 'Stairway To Heaven', 'Going To California' and 'Battle Of Evermore'. In February 1992 a special limited edition promotional copy of the 'Stairway' was released to commemorate the song's 20th anniversary.

With its carefully constructed arrangement, tasteful use of dynamics and the grand climax that gradually fades to black, 'Stairway' has all the attributes most rock songs tend to lack. The band were justly proud of their achievement and Page called it "A glittering thing". After the band had finished their March 1971 Ireland dates, they went on to the small venue trip around England, which finished with a show at the Marquee in London's

Soho. In the packed and overheated club (which had first refused Zeppelin's booking on the grounds that they didn't believe the caller was serious, or indeed that he was Peter Grant), 'Stairway To Heaven' achieved a new kind of intimacy. Whatever the setting and whether played by symphony orchestras or cabaret singers, it reached out to people.

A group called The Far Corporation had a hit with a version in December 1985 which, if nothing else, sparked off fresh interest in a band that had, by then, been woefully neglected for some years. Even when the song was covered years later by Australian comedian Rolf Harris, in a bizarre singalong version, somehow the strength of the tune survived – wobble-board and all. The track was part of an album called 'Stairways To Heaven', consisting of 22 different cover versions of the song by Australian artists. Rolf's groovy version was actually a UK Top 10 hit which he performed on BBC TV's *Top Of The Pops*. Most Zeppelin fans thought it was quite funny once they'd got over the shock and refused to take umbrage, and nor did Plant. "Was I upset about Rolf doing 'Stairway To Heaven'? No, not at all. I'll get me own back. Look who cares? When I get back on the road I'll do a couple of Rolf Harris songs!"

MISTY MOUNTAIN HOP

Here was an early example of John Paul Jones using electric piano on a bright, fast-paced tune which Plant has often revived since its inception. Its dreamy lyrics have a 'stoned hippie' feel, enlivened by a stomping bass drum beat. While it is an apparently simple theme, there is an odd feeling about the phrasing and rhythm. Plant sings rather menacingly: "Why don't you take a look at yourself and describe what you see?" which might possibly be a poke at record reviewers.

Plant has hinted the song was originally devised in honour of a love-in session that took place in London during the hippie era and was broken up by the police.

Overleaf:

John Bonham sticks

it to the world

Said Jimmy Page: "We were just playing around and suddenly I came up with the opening part of 'Misty Mountain Hop' and then we were off. Jonesy put the chords in for the chorus and that would shape it up. We used to work pretty fast."

FOUR STICKS

Heavy processing gives the vocals a strange electronic feel on this controversial piece, which has had both its detractors and supporters. Certainly it has taken on a new light in the wake of subsequent recording developments – what sounded strange and almost inhuman in 1971 now compares favourably with the electronic mixed-up music of the 90s. It has John Bonham playing with four sticks, while Plant offers his customary "Ooh yeahs". Some critics missed the point and called this track "Messy and unrewarding". It is certainly insistent and hypnotic. As Page says: "It was supposed to be abstract." The song was originally recorded by Page and Plant during a visit to India, when they had set off around the world in search of ethnic musical influences beyond the blues.

"We tried different ways of approaching it," said Page, "because it wasn't four sticks to begin with, it was two. The idea was to get this abstract feel. We tried that on numerous occasions and it didn't come off until the day that Bonham had a Double Diamond beer, picked up two sets of four drum sticks and did it again. It was magic. One take and the whole thing had suddenly been made. It was probably because it was physically impossible for Bonham to do another take. But suddenly it happened and that was really great. It was actually done at Island Studios."

Andy Johns found the track very difficult to mix because of the amount of compression used on the drums, and was never happy with the final mix, even though he claimed it was "the best of five or six attempts." The track was later re-done with members of the Bombay Symphony Orchestra in 1972 in a version that has yet to see the light of day. 'Four Sticks' was only once played live by the band, at a gig in Copenhagen, during their 1970 European tour.

GOING TO CALIFORNIA

One of Plant's most attractive melodies, this piece was somewhat influenced by Joni Mitchell, a much-favoured artist who Plant and Page both went to see in concert. When Plant finally met her in the mid-70s he called it one of the great moments in his life. Mitchell had cut a song called 'California' on her album *Blue*.

Originally called 'A Guide To California', it was inspired by tales of earthquakes which constantly threaten the state. But in the song, Plant is apparently searching for a beautiful lady, rather than an earth tremor. He often sang it at concerts during the band's quieter acoustic moments and revived it for a reunion appearance at the 1990 Knebworth Festival.

It developed out of a late-night jam session at Headley Grange – as there were so few distractions at the house, there was nothing much else to do in the evening but get the acoustic guitars out. Jones and Page sat around the log fire and strummed their mandolins while Plant improvized the lyrics. Page, Andy Johns and Peter Grant later flew to California to mix the track at Sunset Sound and, as they landed, an earthquake struck the area, cracking a dam in nearby San Diego.

WHEN THE LEVEE BREAKS

Boom-a-bom-bash!" In an age when drum kits were frequently padded with blankets, and even the cymbals were swathed in masking tape by anxious engineers, John Bonham achieved a miracle when he unleashed the vast and vibrant drum sound that permeates this stunning performance. The producer got the sound, but it was Bonham who played the

Joni Mitchell, who inspired 'Going To California'

sticks. The sheer metronomic intensity of this performance set a new standard for recorded drumming that was only fully appreciated years later, when the 'Bonham sound' was sampled and used on many records during the 80s.

It seems that Bonham was invariably unhappy with the quality of sound he was getting on Zep sessions. After pondering the problem, Page and Andy Johns came up with some suggestions. Bonham and his roadies set up his brand new kit in the hallway at Headley Grange while Johns hung a pair of M160 stereo microphones overhead, placing one on the first floor landing. The sound was further enhanced by feeding it through a guitar echo unit and, says Johns, "compressing it like hell." Bonham kicked in with a walloping bass and snare drum back-beat, creating what Robert Plant succinctly described as a "sex groove" of a kind only Bonham could deliver. The results were fantastic; nobody had ever heard anything like it.

Johns recalls it was the first time Bonham had got a drum sound he really liked. As Page remembers: "We worked on the ambience of the instruments all the way through our albums. I'd been on so many sessions where the drummer was stuck in a booth and he'd be hitting the drums for all he was worth and it would just sound as though he was hitting a cardboard box. I knew the drums had to breathe to get a proper sound. That drum sound is now captured digitally on machines, but we set a trend and it was more fun doing it our way. Once the drums were set up in the hall we got this phenomenal effect and that was going to be the drum sound for 'Levee'. The drum sound actually fired it. As soon as they were set up, that's when we went for it, and it worked. We'd had a couple of attempts before, when it just didn't feel right."

The walls of the building were lined with plaster and there was no furniture to act as a baffle, which also helped create the new effect. Said Johns: "That track marked the first time anyone consciously used just room microphones for drums."

Bonham's slow drag beat perfectly suited the bluesy feel of the piece, which was based on an old song by Memphis Minnie and Kansas Joe McCoy that Plant dug up from his collection. Although the lyrics were ostensibly about the dangers of manmade earthworks collapsing under a river's floodwaters, they could also be construed as a metaphor for sexual desires giving way to a sustained physical onslaught. At least that is the interpretation placed upon them by students of ethnic music and man's carnal appetites, which are not such strange bedfellows as they might seem.

Said Page: "I came up with the guitar riff and Robert sang the words, which were inspired by Memphis Minnie's original version, so we gave her a credit. If you heard the original Memphis Minnie version of this, you wouldn't recognize the two." This is a deliberately ramshackle performance, in which Plant howls like Howlin' Wolf, and the spluttering, shimmering bottleneck guitars and wailing harmonica suggest the humid heat of the Deep South. Their version ends with the still-crackling guitars being switched off for the night and returned to their velvet-lined cases. "I wanted to make his song sound as ominous as possible, and as each new verse comes, there's something new that happens." Page explained that the sound of the vocals changed on each new verse with slight phasing added. "The harp instrumentals were all done with backwards echo on them. At the end the whole effect starts to spiral, with the voice remaining constant in the middle. It only really comes out on headphones. This was very difficult to mix."

'When The Levee Breaks' was rarely played live, beyond a few dates on the 1975 US tour. It was, however, revived on the Page-Plant *Unledded* show.

> " ONCE THE DRUMS WERE SET UP IN THE HALL WE GOT THIS PHENOMENAL EFFECT AND THAT WAS GOING TO BE THE DRUM SOUND FOR 'LEVEE'. THE DRUM SOUND ACTUALLY FIRED IT. AS SOON AS THEY WERE SET UP, THAT'S WHEN WE WENT FOR IT AND IT WORKED. "
>
> JIMMY PAGE

Massive attack as Bonham goes for the 'Levee' sound

5 HOUSES OF THE HOLY

(ATLANTIC K50014) 1973

Houses Of The Holy gained credibility over the years and contains several great works, including 'The Song Remains The Same' and 'The Ocean'. It sparked a fresh bout of Zeppelin mania and topped the world's album charts.

THE SONG REMAINS THE SAME

THE RAIN SONG

OVER THE HILLS AND FAR AWAY

THE CRUNGE

DANCING DAYS

D'YER MAK'ER

NO QUARTER

THE OCEAN

At the start of 1972, 'Black Dog' from *Four Symbols* was roaring up the US singles charts and the band's reputation was at an all-time high. They were still being bugged by press stories about whether they were going to break up, which hinted at dissatisfaction within the ranks, but most such stories were merely an elaboration of the rumours that always attend any media phenomenon.

Led Zeppelin was undoubtedly a fully-fledged supergroup, whether the band members liked it or not, and for the moment they could hardly set a foot wrong. Their albums and singles were devoured by the million and shows sold out as soon as tickets came on stream. But the band needed a rest and avoided too many live appearances throughout 1972, giving them a chance to spend time with wives and girlfriends. In April, Plant's wife Maureen gave birth to their son, Karac. Eventually the group managed to fit in another American tour, and in December they played a couple of British shows, at London's Alexandra Palace.

The first big event of 1973 came on March 26 with the release of their fifth major work, *Houses Of The Holy*. Although it proved to be perhaps the least satisfactory of their string of albums thus far, it immediately went straight to No.1 in both the UK and US charts. In fact, many of the most disputed pieces on the record, like 'The Crunge' and 'D'yer Mak'er', later became highly popular. At the very least they showed the extraordinary diversity of the band's music and the range of their abilities. However, there was a barrage of abuse, notably from America's leading rock critics, who dubbed the new collection of songs "confused". In retrospect, only the critics were confused – the fans had no hesitation in voting the album a success.

Once again there was no title and little information on the elaborate gate-fold sleeve. The front and rear covers showed a group of naked blonde girls climbing up a series of natural stone steps at the Giant's Causeway in Ireland. The inner sleeve revealed another naked figure holding up one of the girls in front of a ruined castle, under a ray of light. It was a rather eerie scene photographed by Aubrey Powell of Hipgnosis, the design team responsible for Pink Floyd's *Dark Side Of The Moon*. The title *Houses Of The Holy* appears in reverse on the inner record bag of the original vinyl release.

It was all a lot more dramatic than the original idea for the album sleeve, which came courtesy of Hipgnosis's Storm Thorgerson. The famed designer presented Jimmy Page with a picture of a green tennis court and a tennis racquet. When Page asked about the significance of this, Storm explained: "Racket – don't you get it?" Page was affronted: "It was a total insult," he said

Although *Houses Of The Holy* was the first Zeppelin album with a complete title, the song itself didn't appear on the album and only turned up later on *Physical Graffiti*. As Zeppelin's regular recording venue, Headley Grange, was unavailable, sessions took place in the spring of 1972 at Stargroves, Mick Jagger's palatial home in Berkshire. The Stones' mobile studio was wheeled into place, presumably accompanied by the Stones' mobile toilet and mobile canteen.

Not all the pre-production work was done at Stargroves. Many of the tracks were prepared beforehand as demos recorded at Page and Jones' own home studios. Such items as 'The Rain Song', 'Over The Hills' and 'No Quarter' were all prepared in this way. The rest of the material was put together on location at Jagger's place and at Olympic Studios, Barnes; mixing also took place at Electric Lady Studios in New York. There was supposed to be so much good stuff coming out of the band at this time that it was held in abeyance for use on later albums. However, Jimmy Page said that when the band went to Stargroves, they didn't have too much planned out: "When we went down there, we had no set ideas. It was simply a matter of getting together and letting it come out. I don't think we ever had any stagnant periods."

Despite the use of the Stones' mobile studio, the sound was not as dramatic as had been achieved at Headley Grange and the album was undoubtedly a much more patchy affair than *Four Symbols*. There was

> **"WHEN WE WENT DOWN THERE WE HAD NO SET IDEAS. IT WAS SIMPLY A MATTER OF GETTING TOGETHER AND LETTING IT COME OUT. I DON'T THINK WE EVER HAD ANY STAGNANT PERIODS. "**
>
> JIMMY PAGE

Arriving on a jet plane. Led Zeppelin travelled everywhere by private 'Starship' during their 1973 US tours

no hallway or staircase to enhance the ambient sound and no ghost in the machine. Nevertheless it had its high spots, notably the first track, 'The Song Remains The Same', which became one of the band's most popular numbers on tour, and featured some of Jimmy Page's most inspired solo work on record.

With recording completed, the band set off in May 1973 for another series of US dates and played to bigger crowds than ever. As the band rampaged through 33 American cities, they flew, not in an airship, but in a hired Boeing 720B – the *Starship* – complete with luxurious lounge and doubtless their own personal cocktail sticks. This was the scene of many a jolly escapade, including the accidental capture of a group of teenage girls who ended up flying to New York with their heroes. As the *Starship* flew the boys into town, their 30-strong army of roadies sweated and laboured with truckloads of equipment. They brought in not only the PA and instruments, but special lighting effects with spinning mirrors, stroboscopes, lasers and smoke generators

put together by Showco, the top stage show managers. It was a costly business but Zeppelin could earn $250,000 for one gig alone, which could be ploughed back into the shows – or Bonham's garage full of hot rods and Page's collection of guitars.

The tour opened at the Atlanta Braves Stadium on May 4 in front of 50,000 fans. This was followed by their show in Tampa, Florida, the next day, in front of 57,000 people. In July, the band played three dates at Madison Square Garden, which were filmed for the subsequent feature movie *The Song Remains The Same*. Director Joe Massott also filmed the band in Boston and Baltimore. He later quit the project, handing it over to another director.

After the New York show the band were robbed of $180,000 from the safe-deposit box at New York's Drake Hotel. The UK's *Financial Times* had just reported that the band stood to make $35 million during 1973, so perhaps the cash wasn't so important. But as John Bonham observed: "If we'd have said we were not upset, they would have thought we were so rich it meant nothing to us, and if we say we're upset about it, they'll say money is all we care about." The money was actually supposed to pay for the hired Boeing and the film crew, so it was an inconvenience. It was also the cause of much panic among the management, and tour manager Richard Cole had to undergo a lie detector test to prove he didn't take the money. The cash was never recovered and the mystery never solved.

Everything Zeppelin did was on a grand scale. The sheer power and success of the band seemed to mesmerize the music industry, although it was also storing up jealousies and resentments. It only needed an unguarded moment to invite a backlash. For the moment Led Zeppelin were kings of rock, bigger, it seemed, than The Beatles or Elvis Presley.

THE SONG REMAINS THE SAME

Led Zeppelin had the remarkable ability to surprise everyone with fresh ideas and arrangements that broke new ground. Just when the critics reckoned they had Zeppelin's music figured, the band came up with something out of the blue, and forced critics to re-evaluate their opinions. This was the case with 'The

The sheer size of Zeppelin's achievement astonished the industry

Song Remains The Same'. It had some indefinable quality that caused a great up-pricking of ears.

Having left listeners with the sound of 'When The Levee Breaks' still rumbling in the distance, Zeppelin now launched into a tune taken at such a tempo it seems to be played at 45 rpm – in fact the vocal track was speeded up to create a special effect. Plant's lyrics describe his feelings about travelling the world from California to Calcutta and finding that music has much the same power everywhere. His voice is given a strange treatment, notably as he sings the phrase "Sing out Hare Hare, dance the Hoochie Koo". He seems to be inhaling helium while undergoing electric shock treatment, possibly showing his oft-mentioned lack of confidence in a desire to cover up the sound of his voice with studio tricks. All nonsense, of course, but despite his noise and bluster he was a remarkably sensitive soul who took every imagined slight personally and took on a scowling despondency when brought down. Whatever inhibitions caused him grief here Plant is shunted along in this song by his bandmates playing at a cracking pace and with a great sense of unity.

The unexpectedly long introduction is like an overture to a rock opera. Guitar tracks pile on top of each other, until the tempo dramatically halves and Plant comes in with the cry "I had a dream – crazy dream". Bonham's drums place accents with all the accuracy of a precision bombing raid, then Jimmy Page rides again with a solo that is almost orthodox in its American-rock-style improvisation. Fans had grown used to Page flying off at tangents, but here he gets stuck into some of the most direct and fiery playing which Robert later described was the work of "genius". The chopped-up backing riff and dancing bass lines from John Paul Jones seem to be

> ## " THE PROBLEM WITH YOUR BAND IS THAT YOU DON'T DO ANY BALLADS. "
>
> GEORGE HARRISON

Is anybody up there? Communing with the spirits in the sky

trying to check the progress of the song, like a speed governor in a high-performance car.

It was initially intended to be an instrumental, which explains the lengthy intro, and when first played its working title was 'The Overture'. When it was played on stage it became known as 'The Campaign', before eventually being bestowed with its more distinguished title.

THE RAIN SONG

A tasteful, melodic performance, so low-key that it's almost the sort of thing you might expect to hear performed by Three Jacks and A Jill at the Ramada Inn. Certainly Plant was in wistful, romantic mood when he penned the lyrics to this soliloquy on the changing moods of love. "This is the springtime of my loving", he intones breathlessly as Page renders a sensitive acoustic accompaniment using a Dan Electro guitar. The use of a Mellotron by John Paul Jones adds an orchestral flavour to the attractive backing. The Mellotron was an early attempt at creating a kind of semi-mechanical synthesizer, using tape loops triggered by a keyboard. It was employed to great effect by bands like Genesis and The Moody Blues, but its use by Zeppelin was a relatively rare occurrence.

The piece ends with Plant's observation that "Upon us all a little rain must fall", the sort of motto usually found hand-stitched and placed upon a bedroom wall. It's said that the motivation for creating this ballad came from a chance conversation with George Harrison, a surprisingly big fan of Led Zeppelin. He was amazed when he discovered Zeppelin played three-hour sets on stage. The most The Beatles ever played live was about 30 minutes! He told John Bonham: "The problem with your band is that you don't do any ballads". This to the ensemble that had just created 'Stairway To Heaven'! Nevertheless, the tune was retained for many of the band's shows between 1973 and 1975, and was performed as a solo piece toward the end of Zeppelin's career.

OVER THE HILLS AND FAR AWAY

A jerky, choppy rhythm breaks up this curious item, with its vaguely inconclusive coda. It only comes to life when Bonham's drums push Plant into singing "Hey lady – you got the love I need". There is plenty of pleasant folk-style guitar work and the main theme is hypnotic, but it doesn't seem to want to go anywhere. According to Plant, the backing tracks were devised first then he came up with some appropriate lyrics. He found it difficult to sing to some of the increasingly complex melody lines, but however it gave him a chance to indulge in his passion for Celtic mythology.

Released as a single in the US in May 1973, 'Over The Hills And Far Away' failed to get into the Top 50. The song was played live before the album was released during their 1972 US tour and was performed at their 1979 Knebworth shows. It was also featured on Jimmy Page's 1988 *Outrider* tour.

"Yes, sir, you may smoke." Bonham calms pre-flight nerves

THE CRUNGE

A song that happened by accident – a happy accident, as far as Zeppelin were concerned, but they weren't prepared for the reaction when it hit sections of the public and the critics. It started with Bonham laying down a funky beat one day in the Stargroves studio – you can hear the engineer George Chkiantz asking Bonham if he's "ready to rock". Then John Paul Jones joins in on bass and Page begins improvising an appropriate James Brown-style guitar rhythm. Robert Plant adds vocals which encapsulate his feelings about favourite artists, from Otis Redding to Wilson Picket. It was the sort of stuff they'd all be playing if they were in a 'covers' band and not Led Zeppelin – playing just for beer money and kicks.

**Robert dances
The Crunge**

Being Led Zeppelin, they had to add their own slant to proceedings and came up with a dance groove that you couldn't dance to! Plant adopts a hipster voice and the swirling, interlocking riffs become ever-more confusing. "Where's the bridge, where's the confounded bridge?" demands the singer, in best posh Long John Baldry tones. If this had stayed as a simple drums-and-bass work-out, Bonham and Jones might have invented a whole new genre 20 years ahead of their time. As it turned out, the whole thing was a bit of a spoof, which some took too seriously.

The band were so enamoured by the idea of creating a new dance craze – The Crunge – that they considered putting some diagrammatic dance steps on the cover to explain how to cope with a beat that crossed over from 'on' to 'off' every few bars. But that would have been more difficult to produce than the seed catalogue design on *Led Zeppelin III*.

Page played a Fender Stratocaster guitar on this track to get a suitable James Brown feel. You can hear him depressing a whammy bar at the end of each phrase. As Page said later: "Bonzo started the groove on 'The Crunge', then John Paul Jones started playing that descending bass line, and I just came in on the rhythm. You can hear the fun we were having". Plant's recollection was similar: "'The Crunge' was amazing because Bonzo and I were just going into the studio and talking Black Country [a Midlands dialect] through the whole thing." The song was never included in the band's set as a full-blown piece, although Page occasionally threw in a few bars of 'The Crunge' riff and Plant linked it with a real James Brown number during shows at the Los Angeles Forum in 1975.

DANCING DAYS

One of the highlights of the album, 'Dancing Days' has a theme that successfully marries both Eastern and rock'n'roll influences. The tune was inspired by an Indian melody the band heard played on a strange instrument during a trip to Bombay. Plant was also influenced by the Indian music he often heard in the area of Birmingham where his girlfriend lived. The

track also features one of Plant's most mystical and yet restrained vocals, held on to a single note for several of its hypnotic choruses. The curse of the squeaking bass drum pedal, noted on 'The Rain Song' and 'Over The Hills And Far Away', returned and managed to escape undetected on a tune that was played live some time before the album was recorded. But this is a minor problem on what is now seen by many Zeppelin fans as one of their most strangely affecting performances.

Recorded at Stargroves and mixed at Electric Lady in New York, Eddie Kramer recalls seeing Page and Plant dancing in single file across the huge lawn outside the house, during the playback, to celebrate the completion of the song. Incidentally, Kramer had to put up with a series of practical jokes during the recording of this – including having various roadies bursting through his bedroom window all night while he was entertaining a new girlfriend. She left hurriedly in the morning.

The song was the first track from *Houses of the Holy* to be selected for radio promotion. This excellent, angular performance benefits by being heard on CD rather than vinyl; Robert's relaxed and untypical vocals flow through much more clearly.

Jones: "How about a long keyboard solo here?"

D'YER MAK'ER

My wife's gone to the West Indies." "Jamaica?" "No, she went of her own accord." Ah yes, a familiar and amusing music hall joke. The reggae beat employed here was not worthy of the band, not because it is reggae, but because they play it with a heavy, crunching beat, when it's supposed to swing.

Robert Plant, always interested and intrigued by different ethnic music forms, thought it was a great wheeze and wanted the number released as a single. Promo copies were issued to radio stations, and the record was released, backed with 'The Crunge'. It went to No.20 in the US Billboard chart in November, 1973. So Plant was right and the critics were wrong; once again Zeppelin were ahead of their time.

Like 'The Crunge' this track was never performed live, although Plant slipped in a few lines during the medley section of their shows. He observed later that critics took the song too seriously, but admitted that it wasn't really reggae, saying "It only works when the Jamaicans do it, not the whiteys."

NO QUARTER

After several disappointing tracks, this was a return to music of quality. 'No Quarter' was pinned together by John Paul Jones, who takes the reins and instils cohesion into the work. His eerie synth and piano work sets up a mood that gives Plant a chance to put his vocal talents to good use. "Close the door, put out the light," he sings mysteriously, his voice processed through some sort of electronic cheese grater. "The dogs of doom are howling more," he warns us later, and reveals that when the winds of Thor are blowing cold, it's time to put on warm underwear, or at the very least "wear steel that's bright and true".

This interesting arrangement is full of pregnant pauses and, with his atmospheric keyboard playing,

Plant gazes out across an ocean of fans

Jones salvages the remains of the album. A jazz-rock groove develops but the suspicion remains that this isn't a Led Zeppelin album proper. It lacks the smack of firm direction, as four people try out their own ideas. Loose, not tight, 'No Quarter' had its origins in a piece tried out at Headley Grange, then slowed down in its final recorded version. It became Jones' major showcase number at live shows from 1973 onwards, including the brilliant Earls Court appearances in 1975, right up until Zeppelin's Knebworth dates in 1979. Robert Plant also featured the arrangement during his own Manic Nirvana tour in 1990. "No quarter" was a pirate's phrase, much used by Robert Newton in his role as Long John Silver and beloved of the late Keith Moon.

THE OCEAN

Bonham counts in the beat in gruff tones: "We've done four already but now we're steady and then they went 1, 2, 3, 4", he intones, with a touch of menace. However, it seems likely he was referring to nothing more sinister than the four albums Zeppelin had already recorded.

'The Ocean' marked a return to form by a band playing purposefully together. The main riff dances around with a hip and a skip, and the elfin quality is heightened by a few bars of "la la" vocals that are imbued with a peculiar air of menace, perhaps because of the Birmingham cadences of the singers. There are a few choruses of really inspired playing, including a superbly jazzy guitar solo from Page, that is greeted by Plant crying out "Oh it's so good". When the band break into a swing tempo, there is a palpable sense of joy all round. "Singing to an ocean, I can hear the oceans roar", sings Plant, using the phrase as an metaphor for the vast sea of living souls that comprised the nightly Zeppelin audience. "Singing songs until the night turns into day", warbles Plant on a number he dedicated to the audience whenever it was played on tour. The main theme is credited partly to John Bonham, but Robert Plant's lyrics also have a personal slant, as the line "Now I'm singing all my songs to the girl who won my heart", was dedicated to his three-year-old daughter, Carmen.

6 PHYSICAL GRAFFITI

(SWAN SONG SSK89400) 1975

The band's first double album proved a true blockbuster. 'Trampled Underfoot' was fresh and dynamic; Page's delicate 'Bron-Yr-Aur' was a delight; but the hypnotic Eastern theme of 'Kashmir' was the band's greatest achievement.

CUSTARD PIE
THE ROVER
IN MY TIME OF DYING
HOUSES OF THE HOLY
TRAMPLED UNDERFOOT
KASHMIR
IN THE LIGHT
BRON-YR-AUR

DOWN BY THE SEASIDE
TEN YEARS GONE
NIGHT FLIGHT
THE WANTON SONG
BOOGIE WITH STU
BLACK COUNTRY WOMAN
SICK AGAIN

It was an agonisingly long wait for Led Zeppelin's next masterwork. The world was moving on at a rate of knots and rock music was changing. There was no doubt that the huge pulling power of the band and their efforts so far had ensured them a place in the history books, but were Zeppelin being left behind? Could they create valid new music? Or as some critics rumbled, was their best work behind them? As it turned out, even better work was about to come. *Physical Graffiti* was a blockbuster. Although not every track was a winner, it proved much stronger than *Houses Of The Holy*. For the first time since their early albums, Zeppelin showed a brazen, all-consuming confidence that spilled over into the elaborate sleeve design.

The *Physical Graffiti* sleeve only really worked on the double LP format, with its acreage of malleable cardboard. It became an instantly recognizable classic rock album cover. Depicting a typical New York brownstone tenement block, it came complete with cut-out windows showing images that could be changed by moving the inner sleeves. There were naked men and flying airships, angels, groupies and nuns, as well as pictures of the band members and their manager, Peter Grant, in all kinds of poses. The medley of surreal scenes included clips from vintage advertisements, scenes from celebrated movies and even glimpses of the 1953 Coronation ceremony. It was surprising what went on behind the roller blinds. Jimmy Page aptly dubbed it "a Peeping Tom's delight". The sleeve was not just a lot of fun; it was indicative of a more focused and organized campaign. There was a title, the name of the band was on the cover and there were proper sleeve credits.

The unexpectedly vast array of tracks included eight songs recorded during 1974 at Headley Grange, using Ronnie Lane's Mobile Studio instead of the Rolling Stones' truck. Work at the Grange had begun in November 1973 but sessions stopped for a while. There was also a selection of seven songs left over from previous sessions going back to the days of *Led Zeppelin III* recorded at Olympic Studios.

Page explained that they had found themselves with much more than the usual 40 minutes required for an album as a result of the extra hours they'd put into the project. "It was the longest album we'd made," Page later recalled. "We had enough stuff for one-and-a-half

LPs, so we figured we'd put out a double and use some of the material we had done previously but never released, like 'Boogie With Stu'."

He revealed that 'Black Country Woman' and 'The Rover' had both been done at the same time as 'D'yer Mak'er'. 'Bron-Yr-Aur' was slotted for *Led Zeppelin III*; 'Down By The Seaside', 'Night Flight' and 'Boogie With Stu' were from sessions intended for their fourth album. Page came up with the powerful title, which was based on the graffiti used on the cover design and the sheer physical energy that goes into making albums.

There was an explanation for the long delay after *Houses Of The Holy*. At the time they made *Physical Graffiti*, the band were undergoing internal problems involving their keyboard and bass player. During the year before its release, John Paul Jones had been considering his future with the group and had thought of leaving. All of this was kept from the public, though occasionally word would leak out, leading to the "Zeppelin to split" rumours which assailed the media and caused outrage whenever they were published. It seemed odd that Jones should want to quit such a successful band. It might have been a bit wearing, having to put up with Bonham and Richard Cole constantly demolishing bedroom furniture, not to mention the long flights, dressing-room sandwiches and bouts of homesickness, but there were compensations: reasonable money, visits to foreign lands and nightly rock'n'roll sessions. Furthermore, Jones had always seemed to accept his low-key role in the band with good grace – he was the quiet one, who did few interviews and was barely noticed on stage while all the attention was on bare-chested Plant and duck-walking Page.

And yet all musicians have their pride and ego – it goes with the territory. Maybe Jones had visions of playing lengthy Hammond organ solos surrounded by a halo of smoke and lights. He eventually developed his own showcase numbers, which helped to redress the balance, but this wasn't the reason behind his desire to leave. In fact he wanted to make a surprising career move and take up a position as choirmaster at Winchester Cathedral. Zeppelin's manager could see that Jones had become exhausted by all the touring and wanted to lead a more settled existence, but urged him to reconsider. Eventually he did, and got back together with the band in the spring of 1974, in time to make a major contribution to the new album. As Jimmy Page once said, 1974 was a year that "didn't happen". In terms of visible, high-profile group activity this may have been true, but the band had been busy enough behind the scenes. It was the year Grant and his men set up Swan Song, the band's own label, after their original contract with Atlantic expired. They had offices in London and New York and a roster of fine artists like Maggie Bell, Bad Company and The Pretty Things. All the band's subsequent albums were released on Swan Song and distributed by Atlantic. At the New York launch party, guests at the Four Seasons restaurant consumed some £10,000-worth of food and drink. It was during the days when the attitude of most record executives was "Expense is no object". However, expense was kept firmly under control at Swan Song's Kings Road, London office, which was kitted out with second-hand furniture from a Salvation Army building. The name of the label came from a long acoustic-guitar instrumental piece which Jimmy had been fooling around with during recording sessions. A semi-classical epic with added vocals, it had no name until somebody asked what it was called. "'Swan Song'" replied Page. It seemed the perfect name for the next album, but in the event it shifted from album to label.

During the summer, work continued on endless mixing sessions, but as the September release date approached it was realized they'd never make it in time. There was the extra problem of work in hand on their movie, *The Song Remains The Same*, which took up a lot of time. Another reason for the slowdown in Zep operations was the simple need to repair the ravages of the past five years. It is rumoured that Robert Plant underwent a secret operation on his vocal cords during this period, which may have accounted for the perceptible change in the timbre of his singing voice later in his career. In the short term, throat operation or not, he couldn't speak for three weeks. Page also needed rest and claimed in interviews that he had returned from his last American tour "a physical and mental wreck". Never the strongest of people, Page needed to build up his stamina to combat the

> ## " THE MUSIC GELLED AMAZINGLY WELL. EVERYONE LOVED PHYSICAL GRAFFITI AND THAT MEANT A LOT. "
>
> ROBERT PLANT

effects of a poor diet, too many late nights and ceaseless travelling.

Physical Graffiti was released in March 1975 and it quickly topped both US and UK charts. The world went mad for Zeppelin, and all five of their previous albums re-entered the US charts – Zeppelin were the first rock act to have six albums in the chart at the same time. Tickets for newly-announced shows sold out within hours as fans besieged box offices. The year began with a couple of European dates in January, followed by the start of their tenth American tour. In May they played their five sold-out four-hour sets at London's Earls Court, illuminated by lights and lasers. These sets were hailed as among the most exciting and satisfying of all shows seen by British fans. As Led Zeppelin unveiled their new album material, the band were clearly at a peak of artistic and commercial success. Everything that happened afterwards seemed to be either an anticlimax, a disappointment or, at the very worst, a tragedy. But in the summer of 1975 the sun still shone on Zeppelin and their new album was received with great acclaim.

Robert Plant explained how they had approached the making of *Graffiti*: "It was a case of getting together and feeling out the moods of each of us when we met up in the studio for the first time in six months. We began as always, playing and fooling around for a couple of days, including our own standards. Slowly we developed a feel which took us into the new material. Some of the stuff came directly from this approach like 'Trampled Underfoot'. Jimmy was the man who was the music. He went away to his house and worked on it a lot and then brought it to the band in its skeletal state. Slowly everybody brought their personalities into it. The music gelled amazingly well. Everyone loved *Physical Graffiti* and that meant a lot."

CUSTARD PIE

Physical is the word – a smack in the teeth for all those detractors who had begun to doubt Led Zeppelin's innate ability. Here was an ultra-tough riff with a raunchy beat that showed the band were back in business. They seemed a bolder, better band, playing together with a clearly-defined sound and a firm sense of direction. No messy beats, no mangled vocals, just a mix of solid drums and guitar which combined to throw a custard pie in the face of a cynical world. If proof was needed that Headley Grange provided the best recording environment, this cut was it. John Paul Jones provided a sprightly electric clavinet riff in the background to a theme that has its roots in Blind Boy Fuller's 1939 recording 'I Want Some Of Your Pie'. Sonny Terry and Brown McGhee had also recorded a song called 'Custard Pie Blues' in 1947. Bukka White's 'Shake 'Em Down' is quoted in the lyrics. Big Joe Williams recorded yet another version, called 'Drop Down Mama', which may have been the inspiration both for Zeppelin's 'Custard Pie' and for Plant's cry of "Drop down!" As Plant's harmonica wails, Page puts his solo through an ARP synthesizer. Strangely enough, this funky rebel-rouser was never played on tour by Zeppelin, but Plant sang a chorus or two during his solo tours in the 80s and Page performed it during his *Outrider* tour.

THE ROVER

Hot on the heels of 'Custard Pie', this extremely raunchy number is pure mid-70s rock. Once again the band can be heard truly playing together, rather than meeting as echoes on bits of salvaged demo tape. It was far removed from 1969-style Led Zeppelin blues, but then times, styles and recording techniques had moved on, and this was a different, more mature and cohesive beast. The kind of heavy rock-metal heard on 'The Rover' inspired many young metal bands to emulate their heroes – during the late 80s it was almost impossible not to trip over Zep soundalike, bands like White Lion and Kingdom Come. Yet surprisingly the piece was first rehearsed as an acoustic blues piece. It was subsequently recorded as a full band number during the *Houses Of The Holy* sessions at Stargroves. It was evidently remixed, with the powerful guitar solo added in 1974, in time for its addition to *Physical Graffiti*. Like many of the mid-period Zeppelin album tracks, it was not played live on stage, although a bootleg CD reveals it was played during rehearsals.

**"Hallelujah!"
Plant with trusty
tambourine**

IN MY TIME
OF DYING

A four-star classic, this 11-minute feat of Zeppelin engineering shows how imagination, wedded to organisation, produces riveting results. A deeply blue guitar introduction ushers in Robert Plant's opening remarks. "In my time of dying..." he sings with a gloomy foreboding, until the mood gives way to a more confident spirit. Violently powerful drums pick up the beat, then drums, bass and guitar simmer and boil as an obsessive riff builds to a shattering climax. This ended side one. Side two, it should be said, contained the greatest sustained set of performances, not just in Zeppelin's own album history, but in the entire annals of rock recording.

The most extraordinary thing is that the best cuts on *Physical Graffiti* have grown in stature with the passing years, making most rock produced in the 90s sound weak and ineffectual. It would also be hard to salvage another album from the 70s that contained quite so much satisfying and innovative music. 'In My Time Of Dying'

'In My Time Of Dying' could be found on Bob Dylan's 1962 debut album

alone would be a highlight of any other band's output; the distinctly live feel shows that this is very much a spontaneous performance. The musicians feed off each other's rising excitement until the controlled routine is in danger of becoming a riot. "That's gotta be the one", says the voice of John Bonham at the end of the take, to which the engineer says, "Come and have a listen".

The tune was based on a traditional song that Dylan played on his first album, *Bob Dylan*, released back in 1962. It is said that the lyrics were from a 1927 Blind Willie Johnson record called 'Jesus Make Up My Dying Bed'. The number was played on the band's 1975 US tour and at Earls Court in London in May of that year when Plant dedicated the number to the Labour Party's Chancellor of the Exchequer, Dennis Healey

Jimmy Page played it with his band on the 1988 *Outrider* tour. He recalls that the song was still being put together when they first recorded it. "It was jammed at the end and we didn't even have a proper way to stop the thing." Page liked this approach because it made the band sound like "a working group". On the other hand, Plant was apparently not too keen on singing 'In My Time Of Dying' after suffering his serious car crash. As he said later: "Why the hell did I sing that song?"

HOUSES OF THE HOLY

The lost track from the album of the same name – if it had been included on the fifth album, it would have a different story in terms of reviews and reaction. This is a highly acceptable piece of work. A clipped beat and an easy riff provides a platform for some of Page's most manic improvisation. A house of the holy is a church, temple or chapel, but in this case the plural term refers to the spiritual aura that Zeppelin felt attended their concerts. Bonham's squeaking drum pedal can be heard again some three minutes into the song. 'Houses' was recorded and mixed at Olympic and Electric Lady studios, during a session that dates back to 1972. Oddly enough, it was never performed live.

TRAMPLED UNDERFOOT

Shock waves spread outwards when this thunderous track was first heard. Led Zeppelin had never played like this before. Sweeping away all memories of 'The Crunge', this was sheer honest-to-goodness funk, played with open-hearted spirit and relentless drive. It was all the more effective for being so completely unexpected. Not that 'Trampled Underfoot' was revolutionary – there was a touch of Stevie Wonder about the groove – but it was full of bounce. Zeppelin just threw caution to the wind and rocked out.

John Paul Jones proved his value, by providing the surging electric piano current that galvanized the rhythm section. John Bonham responded with a backbeat so solid it threatened to punch holes through the floorboards. The staccato riff that went 'beep, beep, deedle eedle eedle beep beep...' was so tight it threatened to weld fingers to strings and keys. The band were delighted and hugely satisfied when they first developed the number out of a simple jam session. Robert Plant later revealed it was one of his all-time Zeppelin favourites. Certainly it caused a sensation when the band played it live at their 1975 Earls Court shows. For years afterwards fans remembered the moment when the piece just took off with a life and momentum of its own. It seemed like the band wanted to go on playing it forever.

Plant's lyrics were based on Robert Johnson's 1936 recording, 'Terraplane Blues' – at least in the sense that they are about using the vocabulary of motor cars as a sexual metaphor. Plant sings something along the lines of "Grease me down... I could lay it on the road, mama, it ain't no sin. Talkin' about love... Mama let me pump your gas... Baby I could rev all night.... come to me for service... let me change your valves..." and so on.

The song was released as a single in the US, where it got to No.38 in the Billboard chart in May 1975. 'Trampled Underfoot' became a staple of all the band's shows after 1975 and Plant sang it on his 1988 *Now And Zen* tour.

KASHMIR

Rolling thunder and a sustained mood of ominous mystery pervade this, the mightiest of all Zeppelin masterworks. Like 'Trampled Underfoot', it seemed to come out of nowhere, defying all past precedents, but it was much more than a simple jam; it was the result of shared experiences and long hours of hard work. Here the band created a musical picture more effective than a thousand album covers. Once again John

Jones's stomping keyboard work galvanised the funky 'Trampled Underfoot'

**Plant wonders if he
should invest in a
double-necked
tambourine**

Bonham excelled. His contributions to 'Kashmir', 'In My Time Of Dying' and 'Trampled Underfoot' served as a greater testament to his technique and style than any number of recorded drum solos. This powerful drama, that suggests a solemn, marching procession of hooded figures, also boasts one of Robert Plant's finest vocals. He sings with a new kind of humility and serious intent. Perhaps this reflected his own state of mind and a growing maturity.

The Eastern flavour and orchestral sound of 'Kashmir' seemed to launch Led Zeppelin into an entirely different direction. Most bands would be in a state of advanced decay by their sixth album. From the evidence of this song alone, here was a group undergoing a complete renaissance. The lyrics were composed by Plant during a holiday in Southern Morocco, a desert kingdom in northwest Africa, which of course is nowhere near Kashmir, which is a disputed territory of south Asia noted for its rice-growing and beautiful mountain scenery. The song was originally called 'Driving To Kashmir', which meant he had a long

way to go. However, the deeper meaning of the song was the strange link between the grandeur and mystical power of Arabian music and the communicative powers of rock.

Jimmy Page had two distinct riffs available on a home demo he'd made with Bonham. The main theme was based on a guitar tuning that he'd used on 'White Summer', 'Black Mountain Side' and the unheard 'Swan Song' theme. When the theme was eventually combined with a John Paul Jones arrangement, the piece burst into seething life. Page's use of strange Moorish-sounding chords, played on a Dan Electro guitar and backed by session string players, ensured that 'Kashmir' fulfilled its Eastern promise.

Plant explained: "The beat came from John. I wrote the lyrics after driving into the Sahara Desert." He had been heading from Goulimine to Tantan in what used to be called the Spanish Sahara. "I kept bumping down a desert track and there was nobody for miles, except a guy on a camel. The whole inspiration for the song came from the fact the road went on and on and on. It was a single-track road which cut neatly through the desert... it looked like you were driving down a channel. I thought, this is great, but one day... Kashmir. That's my Shangri-La."

Jones, Plant and Page all felt it was one of the greatest Zeppelin tracks ever and a highlight of the band's career. As Jones stated, "It's all there, all the elements that defined the band." Plant recalled: "'Kashmir' was tremendous for the mood. A lot of that was down to Bonzo." Page added: "The intensity of 'Kashmir' was such that when we'd done it, we knew that it was something so magnetic, you just couldn't describe what the quality was. It was just Bonzo and myself at Headley Grange at the start. He played the drums and I did the riff and the overdubs which get duplicated by an orchestra at the end, which brought it even more to life. It seemed so ominous. It's nice to go for a mood and know you've pulled it off." Incidentally, by one of those quirks of recording that beset even the most prudent engineers, a ghost of a previous orchestral track that was 'wiped' can be heard spilling faintly into the left stereo channel.

'Kashmir' was first played in Rotterdam, Holland in January 1975, and in every Zeppelin show thereafter. It was also played at the Atlantic Records birthday party show held at Madison Square Garden in the mid-80s, and on the *Unledded* tour of 1995.

IN THE LIGHT

Recorded at Headley Grange using the late Ronnie Lane's mobile studio, 'In The Light' was largely the creation of John Paul Jones, who used a VCS synthesizer. The track was never performed live because Jones, in common with many synthesizer players in the 70s, found it impossible to keep the instrument in tune. The melody was based on another number called 'In The Morning' and was also called 'Take Me Home', which came complete with a different set of lyrics.

Page said: "We knew exactly what the construction of 'In The Light' would be, but nevertheless I had no idea at the time that John Paul was going to come up with such an amazing synthesizer intro. There were also bowed

guitars at the beginning to give a drone effect." The vocals contain rather too many stock cries of "Ooh baby", but the Beatles-ish chord sequence is very attractive.

BRON-YR-AUR

Quite different from 'Bron-Y-Aur Stomp', although this two-minute acoustic guitar instrumental was recorded during sessions for the *Led Zeppelin III* album way back in May 1970 at Island Studios. It's an exquisite piece played seriously, without affectation, and captures Page in a reflective and relaxed mood. The squeaking strings and occasional fluffed notes only add to the

Page bows to public demand

spontaneity of the performance. Here was the self-taught guitarist struggling against fate and the elements and producing musical magic. Page played a Martin guitar tuned to C6, the same tuning used for 'Friends'.

The different spelling of 'Bron-Yr-Aur' has some significance. 'Bron-y-aur' with a small 'y' and 'a' means 'breast of gold' and refers to the beautiful countryside around the town of Machynlleth, near the river Dovey in Wales. 'Bron-yr-Aur' is the name of the 18th century cottage where Robert Plant spent his childhood holidays, and where Plant and Page stayed in 1970 to write the material that appeared on *Led Zeppelin III*. Some Welsh language experts have pointed out that place names shouldn't have hyphens.

The last acoustic piece recorded by Zeppelin, it was hardly ever performed live, but it can be heard on some bootleg albums. It sounds much better on the Led Zeppelin boxed set CD version than it does on vinyl, with or without hyphens.

DOWN BY THE SEASIDE

Another item originally composed during the 'Bron-Yr-Aur' sessions of 1970 and intended to be an acoustic type-ditty, this was finally recorded as an electric version during the sessions that were scheduled for the fourth album. After much debate it was finally deemed 'below standard' and held over. When it came to discussions about material for *Physical Graffiti*, Plant suggested they re-evaluate the tune and include it on the new album. "Everyone laughed when I suggested it," he recalls. Plant sings it with a bow and a curtsy to Neil Young while John Paul Jones' electric piano adds a pleasant country rock touch. The trembling guitar is a real tear-jerker and the waltzy feel is briefly interspersed by an unexpected twist rhythm.

This is one of many Zeppelin experimental snippets never aired on stage – indeed, they could have built a whole show out of songs that had never been performed live.

TEN YEARS GONE

First love is the subject under discussion here. Plant cannot but allow himself a wry smile as he contemplates the destiny of an old girlfriend who had given him an ultimatum, some ten years earlier. She wanted him to give up his music, his career and his fans, and settle down with her to a steady life of suburban contentment – rock'n'roll and Plant's fans won.

Jimmy Page used some 14 guitar tracks to overdub the harmony section on a piece that was first intended to be an instrumental number. Some fans suspect this is the long lost 'Swan Song'. When it was played live during the band's 1977 dates, John Paul Jones employed a unique three-necked guitar to help recreate his wall of sound. The instrument was made for him by guitar technician Andy Manson and was used together with special bass pedals, but it all became too much for Jones to handle and the number was discarded. Said Robert Plant: "'Ten Years Gone' was painstakingly pieced together from sections Jimmy had written. After the tremendous concentration on a song like that, we'd play anything to loosen up. Out of that came 'Trampled Underfoot' and 'Custard Pie'."

NIGHT FLIGHT

Recorded at Headley Grange with the Rolling Stones' mobile, this 1971 composition was never played live, although it was performed during rehearsals for the 1973 US tour, notably at their July 5 gig in Chicago. It has a brisk boogie-rock rhythm with a touch of The Who in the declamatory breaks. Pete Townshend and Keith Moon might have enjoyed putting this on one of their 70s albums. However, Jones' organ sound drops into a pub-rock mode that sounds curiously out of place. Another version of the tune was cut, with extra backing vocals.

THE WANTON SONG

This is a story about sex that Plant delivers with suitably thrusting energy. Wanton can mean maliciously cruel and destructive as well as dissolute, licentious or immoral; a wanton woman is therefore someone to be feared as much as admired.

Jimmy Page employs backwards echo during his solo here and the guitar is put through a Leslie speaker cabinet of the type used to create a Doppler effect with a Hammond organ. Page first began using backward tape echo in The Yardbirds, and when he tried it on the earliest Zeppelin recordings he had to face considerable opposition from 60s technicians who thought it wouldn't work.

'The Wanton Song' came about as the result of a jam session at rehearsals. It was played on some of the 1975 European and American dates before being dropped.

Jones plays bizarre three-necked guitar with just two hands

BOOGIE WITH STU

Stu' was Ian Stewart, the Rolling Stones' broad-chinned road manager and sometime blues pianist, who died in 1985 from a heart attack. He was a much-loved character with a keen interest in jazz and blues, and had actually been a member of The Rolling Stones until image-conscious manager Andrew Oldham decided Stewart wasn't good-looking enough to be in

the public eye. Relegated to work behind the scenes, what Stewart really enjoyed was a chance to get stuck behind a piano and knock out some boogie-woogie.

This jam session was recorded at Headley Grange using the Stones' mobile, and the theme was based on the Richie Valens' 50s hit song, 'Ooh My Head'. The sleeve credits Mrs Valens among the co-composers – a move intended to ensure the late singer's mother received some royalties. Robert Plant cheerfully referred to the 'Head' arrangement as 'Sloppy Drunk' when it was first unveiled. He revealed that he played guitar on the track, while Page played mandolin. However, some special effects were created by Page slapping a guitar synth. Stewart sounds like he's playing a pub piano covered in beer bottles and filled with tin tacks. Laughter greets the final bars of a jolly hand-clapping, foot-stomping rhythm supplied by John Bonham.

BLACK COUNTRY WOMAN

O riginating from a session held in the back garden of Mick Jagger's country home, Stargroves, in April 1972, this was intended for *Houses Of The Holy* and recorded at the same time as 'D'yer Mak'er'. Sub-titled 'Never Ending Doubting Woman Blues', this acoustic, country-style number originally had Plant adding those words as an extra tag line.

The outdoor location is revealed by the roar of an aeroplane flying overhead at the start of the sessions. It's possible to hear engineer Eddie Kramer muttering something like "I'm trying to get this airplane off" to which Plant replies, "No, leave it on." Recording outdoors was always more difficult than it seemed. Once when Plant tried to go outside to sing the song, he was attacked by a flock of angry geese.

Page used a special blues G-tuning on a number that was eventually performed by the band during their 1977 US tour. John Paul Jones was featured on the tune, playing an upright bass in true skiffle fashion.

SICK AGAIN

T he Los Angeles groupie scene was the inspiration for this glam metal rocker, which refers to the heavy competition among girls for the band's favours. As at least two members of the band were married by this time, it was perhaps not the best subject for wide-ranging discussion.

The guitars have a sardonic ring and Plant's vocals are buried deep in the mix, but you can hear him in best Marc Bolan groove talking about "the teenage dream" and "the circus of LA queens". You could imagine the band jamming on this at some sleazy Hollywood bar, wearing feather boas and costume jewellery – and strangely enough, the band did dress up in drag for one night of madness in New Orleans as one of the scenes from the album cover reveals. You can just about hear a suitably sickly cough at the end of the number, which emanates from the drummer, a man whose health was not always in the best condition after a night on the tiles.

The song was performed live on their 1975 and 1977 tour dates but, mourned Robert, who took his writing very seriously, "It was a pity you couldn't hear the lyrics."

Far left and below: "B-b-baby, baby!"

Left: Jammin' with Charlie Watts and pianist Ian Stewart

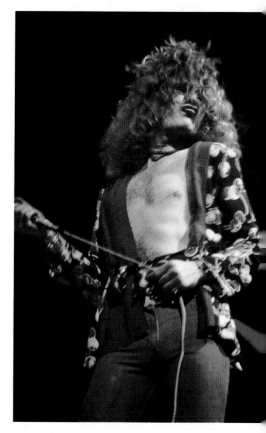

7 PRESENCE

(S W A N   S O N G   S S K   5 9 4 0 2)   1 9 7 6

Robert Plant was still in a plaster cast and recovering from a serious car crash when he recorded *Presence* in Munich. The band played with gritty determination during this difficult period.

ACHILLES LAST STAND

FOR YOUR LIFE

ROYAL ORLEANS

NOBODY'S FAULT BUT MINE

CANDY STORE ROCK

HOTS ON FOR NOWHERE

TEA FOR ONE

During 1975 Led Zeppelin went on the road for their tenth American tour, which proved to be one of their biggest. However, the 26-date marathon was put in jeopardy when Jimmy Page broke a finger on a train door at London's Victoria station. Fortunately it wasn't permanently damaged and the tour opened in Minneapolis on January 18. Even so, it was a painful experience for Page and it meant he couldn't play his showcase number, 'Dazed And Confused', on the first dates.

There was more trouble to come. When the band reached Chicago Stadium, where three shows had been scheduled, Robert Plant was struggling against a bout of 'flu. Shows had to be cancelled to give the singer a chance to recover. A gig at Boston was already cancelled by the authorities because of riots at the ticket queues. Back on the road, Zeppelin were greeted with more uproar in Greensboro, North Carolina, this time when fans without tickets tried to get into the show. Peter Grant drove one of the band's limos to escape from the *melée*, escorted by police with sirens wailing. Grant led the convoy as they drove through three red lights at 70mph on the wrong side of the road. It was his unique way of protecting the boys.

The tour continued through February and ended with three nights at the Los Angeles Forum in March. The music from the new album *Physical Graffiti* had gone down particularly well and as Plant said: "It's like we were on an incredible winning streak." The streak was capped when the band played their sensational London shows at Earls Court in May, performing for three to four hours per night on top form. In July, Page and Plant set off on a trip to Morocco before finalizing plans for their next American tour, due to start in August. The whole world, including South America, now wanted to see the band. It seemed nothing could stop the Zeppelin juggernaut.

But then, on August 4, during his family holiday trip to the Greek island of Rhodes, Robert Plant had a serious crash when his hired car hit a tree. The children in the back seat escaped with minor injuries, but Plant suffered fractures of the ankle and elbow, and his wife, Maureen, fractured her skull. "I looked across at Maureen and thought she had stopped breathing. She was in a terrible state. We didn't have an ambulance to take us to hospital. We were put in an open fruit truck that was so low my leg trailed on the ground," Plant recollected.

Maureen spent several weeks in hospital and Plant was told he would not be able to walk for at least six months. There could certainly be no more touring for a while. The planned world tour, that would have given the band a year abroad for tax purposes, had to be cancelled, and for some time it seemed like the whole future of Led Zeppelin was in jeopardy. After hospital treatment, Plant was flown to Jersey in the Channel Islands to recover, but he remained in considerable pain for many months. Indeed, it seems he was still suffering when the band got back to regular touring again.

In November 1975 the band reassembled at the Musicland Studios in Munich to start work on their seventh album. Page reported that they arrived with hardly any material ready. "We came in with nothing but everything just came pouring out." In fact Page had got together with Plant for a month's stay in Malibu in the US after the trip to Jersey. While the singer was convalescing, some lyrics and a few scraps of tunes had been prepared. 'Achilles Last Stand' was put together during this period, which became one of the highlights of the new album and one of the greatest of all Zeppelin tracks.

The new Plant and Page song seemed to have a lot to do with their nomadic existence as techno gypsies, unable to settle down and live in one particular country, except perhaps England. They might cheerfully have returned home if it hadn't been for their tax status – their accountants warned that it could have disastrous financial consequences. The pair rented a house by the Malibu beach and the sight of attractive girls by the sea was sufficient to help restore Plant's flagging spirits and inspire his songwriting. He spent a lot of time taking solitary strolls along the seashore, supported by a cane, as he contemplated the band's situation and the strange twists of fate that seemed to be dealing them

> **" I LOOKED ACROSS AT MAUREEN AND THOUGHT SHE HAD STOPPED BREATHING. SHE WAS IN A TERRIBLE STATE. WE DIDN'T HAVE AN AMBULANCE TO TAKE US TO HOSPITAL. "**
>
> ROBERT PLANT

lots of bad luck. Even so, he felt much improved and ready for the recording sessions proper.

The pair were joined by John Paul Jones and John Bonham at S.I.R. studios in Hollywood for some early rehearsals, then the band headed for Munich. Plant was still in a plaster cast when he arrived at Musicland, a studio set up in a basement beneath the Arabella Hotel. "It was so strange for me because I was sitting in a soft armchair singing and found myself wiggling inside my cast. But the whole band really wanted to play so a lot of effort was put into the album." Understandably, *Presence* lacked the spirit of *joi de vivre* which sparked most of their previous work, but it boasted 'Achilles Last Stand', which proved to be the band's last major epic before 'Carouselambra' appeared on 1979's *In Through The Out Door.*

> ❝ I THINK WE ONLY WENT OUT TWICE. WE WERE REALLY TOO TIRED TO DO ANYTHING BUT PUT OUR HEADS DOWN. IT WAS LIKE 14 HOURS A DAY, FOR 18 DAYS. ❞
>
> ROBERT PLANT

There was a hint of desperation about the seven tracks they cut in Germany with engineer Keith Harwood. Perhaps their music was affected by their understandable anxiety. The album was also singularly lacking in the variety of sounds and styles that so enlivened previous Zeppelin LPs; there were no acoustic numbers and no experiments with strings. As Page said, this was very much a "guitar album". Nevertheless, it had its exciting moments: 'Candy Store Rock' was pure 50s rock'n'roll fun, and the bluesy 'Tea For One' showed Page on cracking form.

The album was made over a period of three weeks, during which the band spent up to 18 hours a day in the studio. Said Plant: "I think we only went out twice. We were really too tired to do anything but put our heads down. It was like 14 hours a day, for 18 days. *Presence* was like our stand against the elements. We'd left home for 12 months and it seemed that everything was about to crumble. But Jimmy worked like a Trojan. It was his energy that got the album together so quickly – I was not in any physical condition

to hop around inspiring the situation, although I was surprised the vocals were so good. The lyrics were all reflection of the time before and after the accident." Page added: "It was recorded while the band was on the move. We had no base, no home. So there was a lot of aggression in the album. We all agreed that we'd go right back to square one. We just had a few basic structures and the minimum of rehearsal. That's why *Presence* was a testament, like two fingers up to all the things that destroy other bands. There were no acoustic songs, no keyboards and no mellowness. We were under deadline pressure to finish the record and we did the whole thing in those 18 days, with me working up to 20 hours a day. It was up to me to come up with the riffs, which is why it's so guitar heavy."

Page didn't blame anybody for making less than a concerted effort, although he particularly missed input from the keyboard player, and there were generally fewer song ideas than usual from Plant, Jones and Bonham. "We had just finished a tour, Robert was in a cast, so I think everybody was homesick. Our attitude was summed up in the lyrics to 'Tea For One'." The overdubs were finished on November 27. The incoming Rolling Stones had to give up some studio time to allow Zeppelin to complete their work, but it didn't take long and engineer Harwood finished mixing during December. Page recalls that he and Keith Harwood would start mixing and continue until one of them fell asleep: "One of us woke up and carried on going until he passed out again." Mick Jagger expressed amazement that Zeppelin were able to record a whole album so quickly. He told Page it usually took the Stones many months to finish just a few tracks.

The title of Zep's speedy new offering came from the presence that designer Aubrey Powell of Hipgnosis felt sure surrounded the band. The cover art, always so important to Page and often the cause of much argument and delay, was entrusted to Hipgnosis once more. They came up with *The Object*, a piece of twisted black metal that could be construed as some sort of phallic symbol. Carefully superimposed into a selection of stock photographs of American domestic life taken from *Life* magazine, the ambiguous object took on a curiously comic significance. Yet it didn't have much to do with Zeppelin's music, or even the mood of the band. Zeppelin didn't have an awful lot to laugh about after Plant's accident, so the cover, like the title, was intended to present a non-committal stance as the band faced an uncertain future. While they waited for Plant's injuries to heal, they couldn't be sure if they'd ever be able to tour again.

He wanted to call it *Thanksgiving*, in honour of America's national holiday and his own feelings of relief on completing a new album despite his injuries. It was also going to be called *Obelisk*, after the symbol that dotted the cover pictures, but Page ultimately preferred *Presence*. He explained in one interview, "There was no working title for the album. The designer said that when he thought of the group he always thought of power and force. He said: 'There's a definite presence there.' He wanted to call it *Obelisk*, but to me it was more important what was behind the obelisk. The cover is very tongue-in-cheek, a sort of joke on the movie *2001*." Once again, the band's name was missing from the cover, although it was printed on the spine of the gatefold sleeve. This anonymity didn't bother fans or prospective record buyers.

Presence was released in the US on March 31, 1976, and in the UK on April 6. The album immediately went gold on advance orders and went to No.1 in both the UK and US charts after a couple of weeks. In October that year it seemed the band's media dominance was complete, when their full-length feature movie, *The Song Remains The Same*, was given its premiere in both New York and London. The soundtrack double album that accompanied the movie featured extended live versions of 'Dazed And Confused', 'No Quarter', 'Stairway To Heaven', 'Moby Dick' and 'Whole Lotta Love'. The recordings dated back to their 1973 Madison Square gigs and, coming at the end of a tour, the performances were curiously lacking in atmosphere. The version of 'Moby Dick' was not one of Bonham's best performances: there were countless occasions when he played with much more drive and speed. The sound quality wasn't so hot, either, and for many it seemed the soundtrack album – and indeed the movie – was a bit of a white elephant. Many fans believe there are bootleg recordings and archive videos available which give a better insight into the reality of the Zeppelin experience. Certainly, colour film shot in Australia shows that the group really were all that our fond memories would have us believe.

The soundtrack album, released in October 1976, may have detracted from the long-term sales of *Presence*, which wasn't the biggest Zep album, failing to create the same kind of buzz enjoyed by their more successful albums. That said, *Presence* had its own kind of stark, brutal power suited to the late 70s and it undoubtedly featured some of Page's best guitar work – as he said himself: "I think *Presence* was a highly underrated record. It was our best in terms of uninterrupted emotion." After recording the album in three weeks, the group were able to quit freezing-cold Munich and return to Jersey to spend their days in tax exile. At least the break gave Plant and Bonham a chance to jam together in a local nightclub, much to the surprise of revellers who found a detachment of Led Zeppelin rocking out among them. After Christmas 1975 Plant found he could walk unaided and it seemed like good times were gonna come.

> **" PRESENCE WAS A HIGHLY UNDERRATED RECORD. IT WAS OUR BEST IN TERMS OF UNINTERRUPTED EMOTION. "**
>
> JIMMY PAGE

ACHILLES LAST STAND

chilles was the hero of Homer's *Iliad*, the son of Peleus and Thetis. It was Thetis who tried to make Achilles immortal by bathing him in the river Styx. Unfortunately she held him by the heel, which was not immersed and therefore his vulnerable point. When he went to the Trojan wars he was killed by Paris, who wounded him in the heel with an arrow.

Robert Plant sang in a wheelchair during the making of this Zeppelin blockbuster and so, perhaps, felt some empathy with Achilles after his own near-tragic Greek experience with a broken ankle. He has said, however, that the song is concerned with the view from

Plant sits down and takes it easy after his car crash

the top of the Atlas mountains in Southern Morocco. Plant was so excited by the piece that he fell over during the session and nearly exacerbated his injury. "I was hobbling around in the middle of this great track when suddenly enthusiasm got the better of me. I was running to the vocal booth with this orthopaedic crutch when down I went, straight down on the bad foot. There was an almighty crack and a great flash of light and pain and I folded up in agony," he recalled. Page rushed out of the recording booth and held up his old friend. The band helped Plant into a chair while general factotum Richard Cole organized a swift trip to a nearby hospital which almost certainly saved Plant from permanent damage. As it turned out, there were no fresh breaks, which would have been a disaster, as

Plant realized: "If I had opened the fracture I would never have walked again". In the event, he was able to walk unaided by the end of December, 1975, but had to resort to using painkillers.

The lyrics actually refer to the band's wanderings in Africa, rather than Greece, which makes you wonder once again about Page and Plant's map-reading abilities. But this ten-minute piece trundles along with all the furious passage of a Trojan war chariot heading into battle. John Bonham's drums are like horses' hooves, while the guitars clash like flashing swords against clattering shields. The overdubbing facilities available at Musicland enabled Page to build up many layers of sound – Zeppelin had no need for orchestras or string sections when they could create a wall of sound like this. As the battering drums and rumbling bass fade away, we are left with strange, desultory guitar chords, chiming in empty space. For whom the bell tolls, indeed.

'Achilles Last Stand' is a direct descendent of previous Eastern-influenced works, like 'The Song Remains The Same' and 'Kashmir', but has a much harder rock feel. It was achieved quickly, as Page remembers: "I built that track piece by piece and I got it in one night." He used a Gibson Les Paul through a Marshall amplifier to get the sound he wanted. During the planning stages John Paul Jones was quite concerned about Page's proposed solo and said: "This won't work. It's impossible!" Jimmy assured Jones he knew what he was doing. After all, he had been told way back on his earliest albums that backwards tape echo wouldn't work, and he'd always proved his engineers wrong. When the band got back together again for rehearsals for their 1977 tour, this was one of the first numbers they tried out, and it was played consistently during live shows right up until the end of the band. "This number was so intense. It just didn't let up," recalled Page.

FOR YOUR LIFE

 song noted for its bitter, contemplative lyrics from Plant, still traumatized by recent events, but more relevantly, disillusioned with certain aspects of the rock lifestyle. After all, what did fame and fortune mean when you were in pain and separated from your home and family? The normal diversions found on the road suddenly seemed shallow; there had to be more to life.

A rattling tambourine fails to dissipate the doomy mood created by the singer, who seems to deliberately disguise his lyrics. Through the static interference of "Oh, ohs" and twisted enunciation, you can hear Plant sing, "She said – don't you want some cocaine and try a one-night stand?" He later said the song was "a sarcastic dig" at someone he knew and liked in Los Angeles who got sucked into the LA drugs scene. "'For

Your Life' is sort of wagging the finger and saying 'watch it'," explained Plant.

The backing riff has the dramatic quality of a TV cop show theme tune. When guitar and bass play in unison, Page and Jones create a very funky groove that is almost rap style, a decade ahead of its time. Vocally, Plant seems to be struggling – a lemon squeezed dry, as one acerbic critic put it. Certainly lines like "Do it – if you wanna" suggest that a degree of mental and physical exhaustion had beset the once cheery, active youth of yesteryear. Jimmy Page used a blue 1962 Fender Stratocaster guitar for the first time on this piece, which he later used with The Firm. Despite his best efforts, 'For Your Life' doesn't want to take off, and although it got to rehearsal stage, it was never performed in a live setting. It was certainly a million miles from The Yardbirds and 'For Your Love'.

ROYAL ORLEANS

Phil Carson, a long-term associate of Led Zeppelin, says: "Everyone should study the lyrics to 'Royal Orleans'. It's about a member of the band waking up in bed with a drag queen. Did it give him a shock? I don't think so." In fact it's very hard to decipher what Plant is singing about, or who he has in mind. The word 'whiskers' pops up, so we can assume this is the physical characteristic that gives away the bedmate picked up on Bourbon Street.

'Royal Orleans' was a hotel in the French quarter of New Orleans at 621 St Louis Street, a place where the band relaxed and enjoyed life in their own inimitable fashion. They spent a lot of time in gay bars, where they found the drag queens more fun than boring 'straights' and could

> **"EVERYONE SHOULD STUDY THE LYRICS TO 'ROYAL ORLEANS'. IT'S ABOUT A MEMBER OF THE BAND WAKING UP IN BED WITH A DRAG QUEEN. DID IT GIVE HIM A SHOCK? I DON'T THINK SO."**
>
> PHIL CARSON

drink without being hassled. Some authorities have suggested the lyrics refer to a session player known to both Page and Jones. Certainly Plant can be heard singing about "a man I know", so the party could have been someone closer to home.

In fact the band's indefatigable tour manager, Richard Cole, insists that it was one of the band who ended up with a drag queen in his room at The Royal Orleans, without realising the true identity of his guest. Perhaps it was during the moment of discovery that they accidentally set the bed alight with a cigarette, which resulted in the fire brigade being called and all hell breaking loose.

NOBODY'S FAULT BUT MINE

The guitar intro is very bluesy and features Plant singing wordless phrases in tight unison with the lead line. All clever stuff and especially effective when the band blasts into action. "It's nobody's fault but mine!" declares the singer, but adds later, "The devil he told me to roll". There are long, pregnant pauses in the musical narrative, and the way the vocals and Plant's excellent harmonica-playing bounce off the drums recalls the work of Jack Bruce and Ginger Baker of Cream.

Plant really comes on in his 'Wild Man of Blues' role. When he plays his old harmonica with such earthy power you can imagine the mighty Led Zeppelin, kings of stadium rock, back in a small club playing for beer and peanuts. The number doesn't seem too promising at first, but picks up and develops a life of its own. Some crazed solo work from Page enlivens the final chorus or so. The tune was partly inspired by Blind Willie Johnson, who wrote similar lyrics way back in the 20s. In the 70s Led Zeppelin played it on their 1977 US tour and at Knebworth, England, in 1979. Plant also featured the number during his solo tours in the 80s.

CANDY STORE ROCK

The spirits of Elvis, Gene Vincent and Eddie Cochran loom over this rock'n'roller, in which Bonham pushes the beat with commendable zeal. Heavy use of echo give the guitars an authentic 50s flavour as Plant sings from the depth of his plaster cast. The

**Left:
A street in New Orleans, city of fun, mystery and dodgy bars**

Elvis Presley, pioneer hip wiggler. He got to the candy store first

tune was composed in the studio, with Plant putting the lyrics together from fragments of dimly-remembered Elvis Presley records. 'Candy Store Rock' took little more than an hour to compose and was hailed as a great success. Page recorded most of the solos for these tracks during one 14-hour session, hoping to have everything done by the time they had to quit the studio, hence the spirit of urgency. Some have detected the influence of Gene Vincent's guitarist Cliff Gallup on the rockabilly guitar work.

This track was prepared for a live airing but in the event was never played on tour. It was, however, released as a single in the US in June, 1976, backed with 'Royal Orleans', but failed to set the charts alight.

Plant described 'Candy Store Rock' as one of his personal favourites from the album: "This was me trying to be Ral Donner, and the rhythm section was inspired." Chicago-born singer Ral Donner had hits with 'Girl Of My Best Friend' and the chart-topping 'Please Don't Go' way back in 1961. Narrator of the film 'This Is Elvis', he died of cancer in 1984.

> **" THE GUITAR PLAYING ON THIS ALBUM SURPASSED ANYTHING I'D HEARD IN AGES. IT WAS BRILLIANT. "**
>
> ROBERT PLANT

HOTS ON FOR NOWHERE

Another studio creation and written in an hour, it has a dancing beat set to Plant's yelps of "la la la", which sound plain silly on first hearing but begin to make sense as the number grows on the listener with repeated plays. It's a song in the round, rather like "Ring O Roses" and if played by any band other than Led Zeppelin would have received short shrift. As it was, Zep deserved long shrift for trying.

Opposite:

Hots on for

pyromania

The lyrics were written during the band's rehearsals in Malibu and reflected a certain dissatisfaction "with friends who would give me fuck all", who are believed to be Messrs Grant and Page. This callously merry outing has lots of sharp stops for guitar breaks and the drumming is superb. "I really dig it", sings Plant as Bonham hammers him with a series of fills that threaten to set his kit on fire. Page contributes a sizzling final break which must have induced even the most disinterested spectator to ejaculate "Wow". These lesser-known pieces from the tale end of a neglected album are full of surprises. The biggest one was yet to come.

TEA FOR ONE

According to Robert Plant, this track and 'Candy Store Rock' share a common theme in that they explore the subject of loneliness, pain and hurt. Certainly the guitar intro sounds painful, until the tempo slows down for a more relaxed exploration of a slow, bluesy ballad. It develops into one of the band's most tasteful, low-key, sombre and reflective outpourings.

Page and Bonham exchange a wild outburst of passion before returning to *sotto voce* groove. The drummer keeps perfect time on his ride cymbal, while providing the occasional press roll to sustain Page's unusually long guitar solo. It sounds like they are floating on well-oiled casters. As Plant commented: "The guitar playing on this album surpassed anything I'd heard in ages. It was brilliant." The languid mood is deceptive; while Plant sings with a rare show of restraint, the feeling is nonetheless passionate. Forget Fleetwood Mac and Chicken Shack, this is as bluesy as young Brits can get. The mood recalls their other great slow blues epic, 'Since I've Been Loving You' from *Led Zeppelin III*, and reflects a yearning to return to the roots and find out what had happened to them since their days of innocent and carefree youth. More directly, the lyrics came from Plant's increasing sense of homesickness while on the road in the States, exacerbated when he found himself alone in a New York hotel – drinking tea for one.

8 IN THROUGH THE OUT DOOR

(SWAN SONG SSK 59410) 1979

Released shortly after the band's last British appearance at Knebworth in 1979, this final Led Zeppelin studio album convincingly topped charts around the world.

IN THE EVENING

SOUTH BOUND SAUREZ

FOOL IN THE RAIN

HOT DOG

CAROUSELAMBRA

ALL MY LOVE

I'M GONNA CRAWL

By the time Led Zeppelin came to record what would prove to be their last studio album, the rock scene had undergone a radical sea change. Speculation concerning all aspects of Zeppelin activity remained high. At grass roots their fan base remained secure, although in the wake of *Presence* there was less media excitement. The first stirrings of the Sex Pistols and punk rock were being observed during 1976 and the air was heavy with impending revolution. While *Presence* was given a full-page, heavily analytical treatment in the April 10 issue of *Melody Maker*, further back in the pages of the famed British music paper there was one of the first mentions of the Sex Pistols. "Let's hope we hear no more about them", said the reviewer summing up one of their early gigs. He was clearly not anticipating the tidal wave of publicity about to engulf the Sex Pistols, the media and the music industry.

Just when Zeppelin were at a low ebb and uncertain about their future, along came a new wave of bands with a very positive attitude: They were positive that they hated Led Zeppelin and all the bands that preceded them. In retrospect, it was easy to see why new artists felt stifled, frustrated and boxed-in by the sheer weight of the mega bands. Overnight, Zeppelin, Pink Floyd, Yes and Jethro Tull – bands that had filled the stadiums of rock for nearly a decade – were dubbed dinosaurs. Punk rockers blew a blast of foetid air into the faces of the rich and famous and no one was safe. The Clash proudly announced that they'd vomit at the sight of a Zeppelin album.

Yet apart from all the snarling, spitting and abuse, the music The Pistols and The Clash played was barely distinguishable from the pub rock that had been touted as a viable alternative throughout the 70s. Pub rock meant playing the same old rock'n'roll riffs from a pile of beer crates rather than from a stage in a stadium – and it meant playing with less panache. As for punk rock, all it really meant was that young bands could get a foot in the door and hopefully enjoy some of the fame and riches they professed to despise. It was interesting to see that once the chief protagonists of punk had earned sufficient cash, they hastily took up residence in

California, unlike the members of Led Zeppelin who lived at home in England.

Yet Jimmy Page and Robert Plant welcomed the new movement, visited punk clubs and agreed it was time for a change. After all, rock was supposed to be about youthful rebellion. They couldn't help but feel sympathetic to the rising aspirations of an angry and frustrated generation who seemed to think they were missing out on all the fun. But Zeppelin didn't much like the onslaught of verbal abuse which came, less from musicians, but more from critics who had felt enslaved by the all-powerful supergroups and wanted their freedom, too.

Strangely enough, among Zeppelin's loudest detractors during this hostile and turbulent period were people in the music business, A&R men, DJs and promoters, who largely owed their existence to the success of big rock bands. Rather like peasants overturning the statues of a hated dictator in some newly-liberated country, they joined in the great punk revolution and set about destroying icons and reputations. Yet sizeable segments of the public remained loyal to their old favourites and were largely indifferent to the face-pulling iconoclasts. Even when it became almost a punishable offence to admit you liked Led Zeppelin, fans continued to buy their records and celebrated their ongoing infatuation with a band that had changed and affected so many people's lives.

To the chagrin of those who tried to inflict German electronica or punks on the populace, Led Zeppelin continued to win polls, top charts and sell concert tickets. More important still, there were many *arriviste* musicians busy making records who acknowledged their debt to a band that had always been ahead of the game. Once Robert Plant had fully recovered from his 1975 accident, it seemed that Led Zeppelin could at last restore its enthusiasm and momentum.

In April 1977, Led Zeppelin set off on their 11th US tour. At first all seemed well; once again the old hysteria built up and tickets sold out within hours. But instead of this being a time of joy and celebration for fans and the band, the atmosphere turned sour and nasty. On May 6 they played to a crowd of 76,000 in Michigan, breaking the band's attendance record. The same month they received an Ivor Novello Award for their contribution to British music. The establishment had begun to recognize their achievements and Zeppelin's kudos was at an all-time high. Then, backstage during a show at the Oakland Coliseum on July 23, a fight broke out between manager Peter Grant, John Bonham, a Zeppelin bodyguard called John Bindon, and a member of promoter Bill Graham's security staff.

The fight was over the most trivial of matters. One of the security men refused a boy permission to remove Zeppelin's wooden name plate from a caravan for a souvenir. Unfortunately for the security man, it was Peter Grant's son Warren, who had asked for the nameplate and he had apparently been cuffed around the head for asking. This was a signal for violent retribution against the guard by John Bonham who had seen the incident, followed by further punishment meted out by Peter Grant and John Bindon.

Bill Graham called the police and the Zep men were arrested, accused of assault, then freed on bail. The case against them was eventually settled in February, 1978, when they received fines and suspended sentences. But the incident soured the band's relations with America and that country's foremost rock promoter. The States had put up with the Brits rampaging through their hotels and creating havoc, but this was something else.

Worse was soon to come. Just a few days later, on July 26, news came from England that Robert Plant's five-year-old son, Karac, had fallen ill from a viral stomach infection. The next day his condition worsened and he was taken to hospital, but was found dead on arrival. Robert was devastated. He flew straight home to his family and the remaining dates of the US tour were cancelled.

Rumours swiftly spread that after such appalling bad luck, the band would break up. There was no doubt this combination of events left Plant questioning his commitment to the band. But after a year spent quietly recovering from the tragedy, Plant eventually re-emerged to face the world. He sang with friends and local musicians and gradually gained the confidence to return to the public's gaze. Yet he was never quite so sure whether he really wanted to be part of the great game of rock'n'roll. As he told me in 1993, "I sometimes think I could quite easily get up and go, and leave everything, and end up in another part of the world as somebody else. It is possible to leave this persona of a rock'n'roll singer. I've done it before. I think I did it when my boy Karac died in 1977. I left Zeppelin completely. I left the mentality that you need to be a singer. My values changed then."

Plant never likes to be tied down to positive pronouncements about his career moves in interviews and says: "It's just entertainment. It's the music that counts, not the burble that comes out of our mouths. But I was thinking that if I stepped to one side and walked down another street and changed all the phone numbers and moved, it would be quite an interesting phenomenon." After all the shocks and tragedies that seemed to accumulate around Zeppelin, it was no wonder that Plant felt disorientated. He took stock, looked back over his life and wondered where he might go next, if the might of Zeppelin didn't hold him in its thrall. "One could become a teacher, a gardener, or a roadie for another group! There is a certain amount of unreality about being a star and eventually fans lose the plot and move on to something else."

In 1977, however, fans wanted Robert Plant to stay at the head of the group he'd helped create. The media was rife with speculation about the band's future — exaggerated tales of excess, emanating mainly from the US, had clouded their musical achievements, and now came the dismal legacy of violence and tragedy. It was no wonder that the joy seemed to go out of the band. But they hadn't finished yet. In their own eyes and ears, they still had a lot more music to play. Said Jimmy Page vehemently, "There's no question of splitting up. I know Robert wants to work again, and he'll start working at his own pace."

When I spoke to Page in August, 1977, he seemed shattered by events and particularly hurt by suggestions that the band's run of bad luck was

> " I SOMETIMES THINK I COULD QUITE EASILY GET UP AND GO, AND LEAVE EVERYTHING, AND END UP IN ANOTHER PART OF THE WORLD AS SOMEBODY ELSE. "
>
> ROBERT PLANT

caused by karma. "That's really tasteless – its not karma at all. I don't see how the band would merit a karmic attack. All we have ever attempted to do is go out, have a good time and please people." Page talked about the possibility of working on a double album of live material, some of it going back to their 1969 Royal Albert Hall concert, but for most of the following 12 months there was little sign of group activity. Plant and Page popped up at various low-key gigs and jam sessions and, in October, Jones and Bonham took part in Paul McCartney's *Rockestra* sessions at EMI Abbey Road studios. Then in November 1978, the group reassembled for rehearsals in London to prepare for their eighth studio album.

After a two year absence, Led Zeppelin were back to work with *In Through The Out Door*, recorded during three weeks in December at Polar Studios, Stockholm, Sweden. The studio was owned by Sweden's most successful pop group, Abba, who kindly offered their facilities to the world's heaviest band. Zeppelin flew off to Stockholm in search of beer and sympathy. Plant and Page had heard that the studio was of the highest quality and wanted to investigate. Explained Plant: "To trek to Sweden in the middle of winter, the studio had to be good and it was. It was sensational and had just the amount of live sound that we liked. Abba's studio was very easy-going and the rooms beckoned for you to play good stuff and dictate the mood, along with the Swedish beer." Even so, Plant flew back home each weekend to be with his family.

The group was ably assisted during the weekly recording sessions by highly skilled Swedish engineers Leif Masses and Lennart Ostlund. They benefited from a much more relaxed atmosphere than was evident during the *Presence* sessions in Germany. The influence of John Paul Jones was much stronger on the new album than on *Presence* – Jones explained that was simply because he tended to turn up for sessions earlier than the rest of the band. He can be heard nipping in to add strong piano lines to songs like 'South Bound Saurez'.

He was luckier than members of certain other groups, who might find their extra tracks surreptitiously erased by their fellow musicians!

Said Jimmy Page about the new album, "It was a case of wanting to try a new approach to a lot of things. The environment was new and one was practically a prisoner in the studio. It was more like a working project than a recreation ground. I'm not saying we had a job to do, but we knew what we were doing and felt ready, having had some pretty good weeks of playing." In view of the changes in the musical climate, Zeppelin wanted to be seen cutting new ground and not relying on past achievements, so Page encouraged the band to experiment. This resulted in an unexpected samba rhythm being employed on a new song called 'Fool In The Rain', and various keyboard tones being used on an extended arrangement to 'Carouselambra'.

Page later took the tapes back to England and worked on them at his home studio. Then the whole band, except Jones, returned to Polar Studios in February 1979 to complete the final mix. During the coming year the band had proposed playing a full European tour, but in the end decided their only live shows would be in the summer at Knebworth, a huge park in Hertfordshire often used for outdoor shows. That event was promoted by Freddie Bannister, who had put on the Bath Festivals where Zeppelin staged their big breakthroughs in 1969 and 1970.

The Knebworth event, scheduled for August 1979, was announced in May and sent a thrill of expectation through the army of Zeppelin fans. After all, it would be the first time the band had played in Britain since May 1975 and their first appearance anywhere in the world since July 1977. There was a whole new generation who had never actually seen the band and, of course, there were the loyal supporters who had been with them since the start, anxious to see their old heroes once more. Initially only one show was booked, but demand for tickets from all around the world was so huge that a second show was slotted in. The first was held on August 4 with a bill that included Fairport Convention, Chas & Dave, Commander Cody,

> " TO TREK TO SWEDEN IN THE MIDDLE OF WINTER, THE STUDIO HAD TO BE GOOD AND IT WAS. IT WAS SENSATIONAL AND HAD JUST THE AMOUNT OF LIVE SOUND THAT WE LIKED. "
>
> ROBERT PLANT

Southside Johnny and The Asbury Jukes, and Todd Rundgren's Utopia.

Zeppelin played a three-hour show and included 'Stairway To Heaven', 'Rock And Roll', 'Whole Lotta Love' and 'Heartbreaker' among the encores. The second show was held on August 11, when Zep were supported by Keith Richard's New Barbarians. The band played well, but in the darkness of the huge field there seemed to be none of the atmosphere old hands remembered from past events. The newcomers tended to stand and stare, waiting to see what all the fuss was about, and when it came the ovation, were less ecstatic. Robert Plant himself seemed to be unsure of the reaction and their performance, and said guardedly at the end of the last show, "It's been alright."

Part of the problem was the long wait the audience had to endure, first for The New Barbarians to come on, and then for Zeppelin. It seemed the organisers and managers backstage were trying to ensure neither band would out-do the other. Perhaps they were arguing about the running order. In the event, they simply wore out an exhausted audience that had been left standing in an uncomfortable field all day. It would have been much better, musically speaking, if Zeppelin had simply played a season at the Royal Albert Hall. It was a lesson learned by Eric Clapton, whose own Albert Hall concerts proved an annual delight.

Some of the subsequent reviews praised the show, but a Sunday Times correspondent sourly called Zeppelin "the worst band in the world". He was obviously a New Barbarians fan. However, 300,000 people had been given the chance to see the legends in action and judge for themselves.

The album was supposed to be released in time for the Knebworth shows but was a few weeks late. It finally emerged in September 1979. The cover was one of their most elaborate since *Physical Graffiti*. It was presented in six different sleeves which showed various scenes set up in a New Orleans-type bar. It was devised once again by the Hipgnosis team, with assistance from Jimmy Page. He suggested designer Aubrey Powell make a special trip to the States to research a prototype location.

The album's title and band name were missing from the cover but could be found on the spine with the aid of a magnifying glass – a compromise most

record dealers probably appreciated. The actual bar room scene was reproduced at Shepperton film studios in England and showed six different characters, including a boogie pianist, bar tender, and a dude in a white suit and hat enjoying a lonely drink. They were photographed from different angles and it looked like a still-life video shoot. It provided one of rock's most distinctive and collectible sleeves. A final clever touch was to introduce an area of the picture that appeared to have been wiped clean of the bar room's smoke and grime. While the sleeve signified a band getting back to its roots with a touch of fresh ideas, the title *In Through The Out Door* referred to the fact that, as Page explained, "It's the hardest way to get back in." Others have since suggested it is a phrase familiar within the gay community, so it could be a double in (or out) joke.

At Peter Grant's suggestion, the album was distributed in plain brown paper wrappers so that nobody knew which version of the sleeve they'd be getting. Presumably the most dedicated fans would spend their lives buying Led Zeppelin albums in the hope of getting the full set. Certainly it sold four million copies in the US alone and topped both US and UK charts for weeks. It also went to No.1 in the album charts of countries that included Australia, Japan, New Zealand and Australia. Such was the excitement generated in America, always the band's biggest market, Atlantic records found they were selling all of the back catalogue. In the end, all of Led Zeppelin's albums were scattered across the Billboard chart at the same time.

In December 1979, Robert Plant, John Paul Jones and John Bonham made a guest appearance in an all-star line up at the *Rock For Kampuchea* concert held at London's Odeon, Hammersmith. Everyone seemed full of peace and love at Christmas-time. At the start of the new decade, all seemed well for the veteran band who had survived so many traumas and triumphs during the previous ten years. In February 1980 'Fool In The Rain', a cut from *In Through The Out Door*, got to No.21 in the US Billboard chart. Then in May the band announced they would make a return trip to Europe. The public sat back and savoured the music on the new album, expecting that during 1980 they'd get another chance to see their favourites, blasting back on stage.

IN THE EVENING

Strange, spooky sounds launch a piece that suddenly leaps from the speakers as we hear a band emerging from the audio fog of the 70s. The new technology available at Abba's Polar studios gave Zeppelin a real presence and depth they had only managed to get in the past by recording in stairwells and the depths of ancient manor houses. The guitar and keyboards have a very modern sound that foreshadows 80s techno-rock. Indeed the band were in advance of their contemporaries like Yes in updating and modernizing. So successful were they in their efforts to restructure, a few desultory passages of blues guitar heard here seem almost out of place in the environment of a sophisticated pop arrangement.

The main riff is a killer and there are all the unexpected twists and changes only Zeppelin would dare put into what is otherwise a basic hit single

John Paul Jones comes 'In Through The Out Door'

FOOL IN THE RAIN

John Bonham employs an unusually highly tuned snare drum sound on a lengthy number that shows the band becoming ever-more adventurous. A kind of Tex Mex feel gives way to a samba rhythm launched by the effervescent piano of Jones. Who would have thought Zeppelin could play like this? It certainly has nothing to do with punk, so the theory of their being influenced by the Sex Pistols flies gracefully out of the window. Plant's voice is greatly improved over his performance on *Presence*.

The choice of samba rhythm was influenced by the Latin music heard on TV during the coverage of the 1978 World Cup football matches then being played in Argentina. Robert Plant, who pushed through his demands for greater musical flexibility, later observed that it was not intended to be an attempt to emulate Carlos Santana. The band cut several different versions of the song. Surprisingly, in view of this massive stylistic shift, 'Fool In The Rain' became a hit in the States, where it got to No.21 in the Billboard charts in January, 1980. Coming at the end of their career, their last chart hit was never played live.

format. It's certainly half a league onwards from 'Bron-Yr-Aur'. Although John Paul Jones put his stamp on 'In The Evening', the introduction sees Jimmy Page using his old violin bow on the intro (crowds cheered this when he played the number at their Knebworth shows). He also utilizes the Gizmotron, a guitar device invented by Lol Creme and Kevin Godley of 10cc fame, to produce and increase distortion. It's believed to be responsible for the peculiar slamming effect heard during the solo.

In the heartfelt lyrics, Plant muses about the pain and grief that people go through in life and the fact that all the success and riches in the world cannot alleviate it. "You can turn away from fortune because that's all that's left to you... It's lonely at the bottom... It's dizzy at the top."

SOUTH BOUND SAUREZ

A perky boogie-rocker set up by the itchy-fingered piano playing of John Paul Jones, which Plant gets stuck into with throaty gusto. A good-time New Orleans feeling permeates the piece, and while Page offers some nice background riffs, his solo is so erratic it practically stumbles through the out door. However, he often insisted that he preferred to leave in any mistakes in his guitar playing, rather than embark on an unrealistic search for perfection. Certainly the odd missed note and squeaky string adds to the drama or pathos of a piece. Bonham was on top form on this one and his bass drum pedal works overtime at what proves a demanding tempo.

A Jones-Plant composition, the title was incorrectly spelt on the label – it should have been *Suarez*, a Spanish word for party. Many thought it must refer to a bus trip to a little-known Mexican village, but it was in fact a celebration – of a celebration.

Left:
Neither dazed nor confused, Page is clearly in control of both instrument and audience

Overleaf:
A flying leap for freedom. Led Zeppelin at the peak of their powers

Jones heads south

It is said that another passion was one of the female citizens of that fair state. Plant fantasizes about a girl who disappears after taking a Greyhound bus. "I searched the town... she took my heart, she took my keys... I'll never go to Texas anymore." More prosaically, 'Hot Dog' is also dedicated to top American tour organizers Showco and their indefatigable road crew.

The tune began life at rehearsals in London. A rarely-seen promo video was made of the song, making use of live footage shot at Knebworth. It was intended for showing at record stores across the States.

CAROUSELAMBRA

A remarkable piece of cutting-edge-of-the-80s pop-rock, 'Carouselambra' showed how Zeppelin might have developed during the next decade. It has all the latest sounds, a majestic keyboard riff and some of Bonham's firmest, most authoritative drumming setting a rock-solid tempo – no need for click tracks or drum machines here. Shamefully overlooked at the time, even now it sounds fresh and exciting and could be a huge hit if revived by a currently popular band.

The ten-minute odyssey pauses unexpectedly half-way through for Page to play some haunting power chords using a Gibson double-neck guitar – and the Gizmotron was also rolled out. The sharp-tongued keyboards spark a return to the crisper tempo and this is a whole new Led Zeppelin in action. The lyrics are largely beyond comprehension and are left open to interpretation. Plant proclaimed that they deliberately hid a mystical intention aimed at a specific person who will one day discover their meaning.

John Paul Jones is in the driving seat of a piece that was originally assembled during rehearsals at Clearwell Castle in the spring of 1978. There are enough ideas and tones here to create an entire album of ambient music. Lambasted on release by sections of the rock press, it can be seen more than a decade later as one of Zeppelin's last classics. This was a new Led Zeppelin taking shape before the eyes

HOT DOG

A n audible count leads into the most cheerful good-time number Led Zeppelin ever cut, on which they seemed to throw all caution to the winds and indulge in a bit of fun. They needed it after all the bad luck and trouble they'd endured.

Page falters fractionally on his finger-lickin' intro, but the piano and drums join forces like a bar room brawl ready to swig pitchers of beer and toss horse shoes all night long. If ever there was a full-scale hootenanny, this was it. Plant called the number a tribute to Texas and hillbilly, another of his great musical passions being the genre known as Rockabilly.

Jones gives 'All My Love'

of a populace blinded by over-familiarity. If the band had been able to continue along this path, they would have been able to create another eight great albums in the 80s.

ALL MY LOVE

Keyboards introduce a simple pop song, written by John Paul Jones and Robert Plant, that shows yet another facet of the band's ability. It's one of the few Zeppelin songs that does not have a Page composer credit and he plays with perfunctory professionalism, as if he was on somebody else's session. Jones' excellent synth solo has a classical pop feel. While not unpleasant, it's almost as if both musicians were unconsciously harking back to their roots, when they provided the backing for such artists as Herman, Donovan and the stars of the 60s. The tune even changes key for the final chorus, in true pop ballad fashion. Plant's vocals show a degree of maturity, with less reliance on "Ooh yeahs" – it is the kind of material he began to develop on his later solo albums.

'All My Love' may have been a tribute to Karac, Plant's son, as he sings "He is a feather in the wind". But on a strictly musical judgement Jimmy Page later professed disquiet at the direction of the track and commented: "It wasn't us."

I'M GONNA CRAWL

Page may have taken a back seat on the previous track, but here he reasserts his authority – and presence. Recorded at Polar Studios and mixed at Page's home studio in Plumpton, this is an immensely sad performance, in terms of its immediate impact and in the light of subsequent events. John Paul Jones is the foremost composer of a piece provisionally intended to recreate the mood of the 60s soul-blues classics created by such singers as Otis Redding and Wilson Pickett.

Page's doleful guitar solo is an outstanding feature of a cocktail bar-type ballad. Plant also gives a wonderful performance bestride an imaginary bar stool, mulling over a slow torch song in a style that owes as much to Mae West as it does Wilson Pickett. He tells how a girl "drives me crazy... she's the apple of my eye. I love that little lady. I got to be her fool." John Bonham later proclaimed that it was one of the best vocal performances that Plant had ever given. Plant, Page, Jones and Bonham sweep grandly through a piece that history proved was Led Zeppelin's swan song.

Below: "Phew – rock'n'roll!" Overleaf: Plant and Page – a whole lotta love

9 CODA

(SWAN SONG A0051) 1982

WE'RE GONNA GROOVE

POOR TOM

I CAN'T QUIT YOU BABY

WALTER'S WALK

OZONE BABY

DARLENE

BONZO'S MONTREAUX

WEARING AND TEARING

When John Bonham died, the group died with him. It was a sad end to the Led Zeppelin saga, but *Coda* helped fans temper their loss by providing rare bonus items culled from the archives.

ollowing the excitement of Led Zeppelin's Knebworth shows in August 1979, it seemed that their bad luck and ill health was over – the worst was surely behind them. They had made a well-received album and their shows were met with great acclaim. Now they planned to embark on a full-scale European tour, followed by a long-awaited return to America.

In April 1980 they began rehearsals at London's Rainbow Theatre, but were forced to move to the New Victoria Cinema as they attempted to maintain a cloak of secrecy. In June they set off to Germany to play their first European tour since March 1973. Zeppelin's new, two-and-a-half-hour show included numbers from most eras of their career with a selection of three songs from their last album. The 14-date Zeppelin Over Europe 80 tour kicked off at the huge Westfalenhalle, Dortmund, on June 17. Many German fans recall that the band were not on their best form at this time, but they were pleased to see them anyway.

The entourage trundled off to Holland and Austria then went back to Germany for a final show in Berlin on July 7. It was just like old times, except that one show at Nuremberg had to be cancelled after only three numbers, when Bonham collapsed on stage suffering from physical exhaustion. The band were generally in a good mood and, despite the Nuremberg incident, Bonham seemed very pleased with the way the tour had gone. He said later: "There were so many things that could have gone wrong. It was a bit of a gamble, this one, but it's worked really well."

Simon Kirke, drummer with Free and Bad Company, was a close friend of the band. One night on the tour, Bonham invited him to sit in. Simon remembers: "Bonzo and I did a duet. We did 'Whole Lotta Love' and we had two kits set up on stage. It's quite a complex arrangement, a whole 12-minute piece. So Bonzo says to me, banging on his knees: 'Right, we do this, got that? Right'. Then Pagey takes over, 'Bomp, bomp – got that? Fookin' great.' It was all done on the knees in the hotel room before we went on stage. I dunno how but I got through to the end. Hearing those opening notes was the heaviest thing I've ever heard, and then of course he died just a month or so later. Yet John was fine when I last saw him."

The intention was for the band to get into shape before the return to the US – they had not set foot there since the *debacle* of the 1977 tour. There's no doubt John Bonham was feeling nervous about the impending trip to the States and may well have wondered what sort of reception he would get after the Oakland incident. In the event, neither Bonham nor Zeppelin returned to America. In September, after a summer holiday, the group returned to England and began rehearsals for the proposed tour of Canada and the US, which was scheduled to open in Montreal on October 17. They decided to rehearse at Jimmy Page's home, the Old Mill House in Windsor, which Page had recently bought from movie actor Michael Caine.

The band arrived on September 24 and, for some reason, Bonham began drinking heavily during the afternoon at a nearby pub. He got locked into downing shots of vodka and orange and, on his return to the house, began topping them up with double vodkas. Bonham made it clear that he was not happy at the prospect of being away in America for a 19-date tour. He collapsed around midnight and was put to bed by Page's chauffeur, who covered him with a blanket and left him to sleep it off. By the following afternoon (September 25, 1980), Bonham still hadn't stirred from his room, so John Paul Jones and roadie Benji Le Fevre tried to wake him but discovered that he had stopped breathing.

All attempts at resuscitation failed and, when an ambulance crew arrived, it was too late. John Henry Bonham, aged 32, was dead. His colleagues were stunned. Plant naturally was the most upset – he and Bonham had been friends since they were teenagers. At the inquest, held on October 8, it was revealed that Bonham had died in the same fashion as Jimi Hendrix, from asphyxiation as a result of inhaling his own vomit. His funeral was held at Rushock Parish Church, Worcestershire, on October 10.

The news rapidly flashed around the world to Zeppelin colleagues, friends and fans. The story made headlines in the press and on radio and TV. Speculation about the band's future was rife. At first it was thought that Zeppelin might try to carry on and recruit a new drummer – such names as Cozy Powell and Carmine Appice were put forward as possible contenders – but no one could really replace the big man with the big heart and the big sound. On December 4 the announcement was made that Led Zeppelin had finally broken up. A brief statement from the band, issued through Swan Song, read: "The loss of our dear friend, and the deep respect we have for his family, together with the sense of undivided harmony felt by ourselves and our manager, have led us to decide that we could not continue as we were."

Once the shock of his death began to abate, many began to wonder why Bonham should have got into such a state about the impending American tour. It all pointed to his growing desire to spend more time at home and less on the road: he'd been playing heavy rock'n'roll drums for years and he was getting tired. On the last album his drumming had seemed as sharp as ever, but touring was a big drain on his energy and stamina – in the interests of conserving energy he'd dropped the big drum solos from the band's act, but he knew that his role was vital in keeping the Zeppelin flag flying. It was Bonham who had to charge up their great blockbuster numbers and bring his sense of dynamics to their arrangements.

In happier times he'd chatted about his role in Zeppelin. He confided his inner fears but expressed a great pride in the band, recalling that life was tough when Led Zeppelin first hit the road. "I remember in the early days when we played six nights a week for a month and I was doing my long drum solo every night. My hands were covered in blisters. We once did six tours of America in 15 months."

It seems strange that Bonham is frequently depicted as some kind of rock monster. Certainly, tales of his exploits are legion, but deep down Bonham was a generous, warm-hearted and kind individual. He was also prone to stage fright. "My

> ## " THE LOSS OF OUR DEAR FRIEND, AND THE DEEP RESPECT WE HAVE FOR HIS FAMILY, TOGETHER WITH THE SENSE OF UNDIVIDED HARMONY FELT BY OURSELVES AND OUR MANAGER, HAVE LED US TO DECIDE THAT WE COULD NOT CONTINUE AS WE WERE. "
>
> LED ZEPPELIN

nerves before a gig got worse; I had terrible bad nerves all the time. Once we started into 'Rock And Roll' I was fine. I just couldn't stand sitting around and worrying about playing badly and then getting pissed off at myself. If I play well... I feel great. I dare not drink before a gig because I'll get tired and blow it. So I have to sit drinking tea in a caravan with everybody saying 'Far out, man!'"

It was undoubtedly boredom and impatience that led to Bonham's more celebrated exploits, but it was also high spirits and good fun. One of his most famous episodes was the lost afternoon when Bonham and blues-guitarist friend, Stan Webb, began drinking at a Soho pub, The Coach and Horses. They started downing glasses of vodka and scotch – a powerful brew – and plotted a series of wild schemes. One of them involved capturing Led Zeppelin's publicist, Bill Harry. They were going to tie him up with a rope then hang him upside-down out of his office window but, fortunately for Harry, he got wind of the plan and fled the scene. Thwarted by Harry's escape, the pair set upon the managing director of a record company and tied him up to his chair with sticky tape until he was bound head to foot like a mummy, then dumped him helpless on the pavement in Oxford Street.

The sight of the mummy gave them an idea and Bonham and Webb dashed off to a theatrical costumiers in Covent Garden. They hired a set of Arab outfits and blacked their faces with make-up. Bonham telephoned the Mayfair Hotel and hired the sumptuous Maharajah Suite for the afternoon. Hotel porters saluted as the fake princes arrived by taxi and took over the room filled with priceless furniture, rich tapestries and furnished with a stuffed tiger. Once inside the suite, Bonham and chums ordered 50 steaks, which were sent flying around the room. There was some damage to the tiger and the furniture, and the party were ejected from the building. Thereafter Bonham was banned from the Mayfair and all the major hotels in London. The wandering Arabs, by now somewhat dejected, ended up at The Speakeasy, a popular rock star's night club. Nobody was fooled by the costumes or the make-up and they were greeted with cries of "Oh no – it's Bonzo!"

Despite the bouts of rock'n'roll excess, Bonham was far happier at home on the farm in Worcestershire, which he bought in 1972. He kept prize sheep and a herd of cattle which grazed on several hundred acres. It amused him to mix with the landed gentry, including the local huntsmen, who he reported were usually "pickled in port on their saddles!" His home was a welcome retreat from the battlefields of rock, although he liked to listen to music, playing a wide selection of records. In the lounge his son, Jason, had a tiny drumkit set up. Many years later, Jason Bonham became a respected drummer and band leader in his own right. He learnt his lessons well – from the source. Said Simon Kirke after Bonham's death: "I felt very privileged to have known Bonzo. We were roughly the same age and we were each other's fans. He was my all-time favourite drummer and he was the best. There was no one within a mile of Bonzo."

When Led Zeppelin broke up it seemed like a tragic end to the rock'n'roll era. Most of the great bands and artists had either gone or were just hollow travesties of their former selves; many had been ruined by drink and drugs. It was two years later, on November 19, 1982, that the tenth and final Led Zeppelin album, *Coda*, appeared with little fanfare. A dictionary definition of the word 'coda' states: "The final, sometimes inessential part of a musical structure." More commonly, it means a tag at the end of a tune. The group's Swan Song contract with Atlantic called for five albums to be delivered. As the remaining members of the band could not produce a new Zeppelin album without John Bonham, they had to delve into the archives and find material suitable for one last hurrah.

But this was no bad thing. Page had often talked about doing a retrospective live album, taking the best of the recordings from the previous 12 years of the band's career; now he had a chance to put this idea into practice. In the event, *Coda* was a rather odd mixture – anybody expecting an unheard new classic along the lines of a 'Whole Lotta Love' or 'Achilles Last Stand' was due for a disappointment. However, it proved to be an attractive album, in the sense that everything on it was a bonus. It was enough just to be able to hear the band in action once more, whatever the sources and standards. In fact, there were some excellent performances, including: a brilliant sound-check version of their classic blues 'I Can't Quit You Baby'; a raunchy number called 'Darlene'; a

resurrected John Bonham drum solo; and the ultimate punk rave-up, 'Wearing And Tearing'.

In all there were eight songs from the years 1969, 1970, 1972, 1976 and 1978. Page found all these tapes at his recording studio in Berkshire and spent most of the summer of 1981 pulling them together. He had been working on the soundtrack for Michael Winner's movie *Death Wish 2* but, when that was completed, he got down to sifting through the old Zeppelin material. It was a labour of love and he brought in Plant and Jones to help out with overdubs. Once completed, the album's release was delayed for a while until Plant's own solo album, *Pictures At Eleven*, was safely underway.

The *Coda* album sleeve was a simple affair in grey and green. The gatefold opened to reveal a selection of band pictures from 1969 to 1979, including colour shots from Bath Festival (1970) and Knebworth (1979). There were no symbols, no hidden messages and no bizarre designs, apart from an insert picture of ten flying black discs on the back cover. This was a cause for some debate among fans. Were they aerial views of crop circles, UFO landing sites in the Mexican desert, or simply LP discs representing the ten Led Zeppelin albums? "Assorted images by Hipgnosis" was the most likely explanation provided by the sleeve credits.

It was a dignified last exit, but very low-key. There was hardly any advertising or promotion – fans were lucky if they spotted posters in the street announcing the album's arrival. Even so, despite the antipathy towards the band from a music press preoccupied with the new music acts of the 80s (including such groups as Bucks Fizz and The Goombay Dance Band), Led Zeppelin's new album got to No.4 in the UK and reached No.6 in the US Billboard album chart. However, it was a sign of the changing times that fans soon found copies of *Coda* on sale in bargain bins in London's Oxford Street.

> " WE WERE ROUGHLY THE SAME AGE AND WE WERE EACH OTHER'S FANS. HE WAS MY ALL TIME FAVOURITE DRUMMER AND HE WAS THE BEST. THERE WAS NO ONE WITHIN A MILE OF BONZO. "
>
> SIMON KIRKE

WE'RE GONNA GROOVE

This provides a fascinating glimpse back into the earliest days of Zeppelin. Here is a track recorded at Morgan Studios, London, on June 25, 1969, at a time when the band had just finished a five-date British tour and were due to play at Bath Festival. Their schedule also included a recording session for BBC radio and appearances at London's Royal Albert Hall.

The tune is credited to soul giant Ben E King and James Bethea and is taken at a fast pace, with Plant in apparently angry, declaiming mood, although the lyrics suggest that when his baby returns from a recent trip on the railroad, he plans to raise a suitably groovy family. Some sub-octivider guitar effects were added later during mixing sessions at Page's Plumpton Sol studio in 1982. 'We're Gonna Groove' was intended to be used on *Led Zeppelin II* but didn't make it onto the album, instead serving as an opening number on their early 1970 tour dates.

Blowing the blues. On stage at London's Royal Albert Hall, 1969

POOR TOM

heavy New Orleans-style shuffle rhythm, which is much harder to play than it sounds, forms the basis of this highly distinctive semi-acoustic cut that was recorded at Olympic Studios, Barnes, in June 1970. Engineered by Andy Johns, it is one of the tracks that didn't survive the selection process for *Led Zeppelin III* and was never performed live, although it had the credentials of having been written during the famous trip to Bron-y-Aur. Plant provides a traditional blues treatment, along with some fine harmonica playing.

'Poor Tom' is a heart-rending tale of old Tom, who had worked hard all his life and is apparently happily married, until he makes an appalling discovery and gets into dire trouble as a consequence. Poor Tom – the seventh son – discovers that his wife, Ellie May, is running around and playing games while he's away at work. As a result, he gets hold of a gun and wreaks vengeance upon her, resulting in more than a custodial sentence. Sings Plant, "Poor Tom... you gotta die for what you've done".

I CAN'T QUIT YOU BABY

Worth the price of the album alone, this is a splendid performance by any standards. The band are captured during a soundcheck at the Royal Albert Hall, playing their tribute to composer Willie Dixon with fire and panache. The great thing is that here is a band, oblivious to the surroundings, playing for themselves. There's no audience, apart from a few blokes sweeping up cigarette butts and roadies humping gear. Up there on the stage are Robert Plant, Jimmy Page, John Paul Jones and John Bonham getting stuck into the blues.

The day this was recorded – January 9, 1970 – Zeppelin were due to be filmed for a proposed documentary, so a mobile truck was installed outside the Albert Hall, which accounts for the superb sound quality.

This is a stronger version of 'I Can't Quit You Baby' than appears on the first album. Page's solo is cleaner and he cunningly drops down the volume, rudely interrupted by Bonham crashing in with a shattering drum break.

WALTER'S WALK

oogie-rock with added angst. Plant offers a brace of "Ooh yeahs" as he describes how he is trying hard to change his ways but "can't let go". A

song of love, anguish and tears develops as he sings "I'm walking the floor over you", while Page adds a violent, energetic, guitar solo. There is too much echo on the vocals but it adds to the sense of doomed love.

The piece was recorded in May 1972 during sessions at Mick Jagger's Stargroves studios in Berkshire, using the Rolling Stones' mobile studio. Eddie Kramer was in charge of engineering and the number was originally intended for the *Houses Of The Holy* album. A strangely muddy sound pervades the piece, which lacks a strong melody. Some experts have suggested this was only ever a backing track, updated later for inclusion in *Coda*. The tune was based on a riff that Page had worked up during performances of 'Dazed And Confused' when the band were on tour in the mid-70s.

"I can't quit you baby!"

OZONE BABY

An interesting item from the Polar Studios sessions in Stockholm, recorded on November 14, 1978, and engineered by Leif Masses, this is very much a structured pop song, composed by Page and Plant and built over a strong bass guitar line. Plant tells how he hears his girl knocking at his door with a cry of "I've been saving this for ya honey". However, it is too late for her to be his honey as he is tired of her doing "the things that you do". He adds "I don't want you ringing my bell" and threatens to go into "the darkness and sail away".

It's not too surprising that 'Ozone Baby' didn't make it onto *In Through The Out Door*. The hook line – "My own true love" – is somewhat trite, it has to be said. Even so, it might have made a hit if Zeppelin had disguised themselves as a Swedish pop group for the day.

DARLENE

An outtake from the Polar Studios sessions for *In Through The Out Door*, the track was recorded on November 16, 1978, and was a much better piece of work than was featured on the 1993 boxed CD set. The song grows in stature with repeated plays and has a strong rock'n'roll feel, enhanced by the busy piano work of Jones. Few rock bands of Zeppelin's ilk were so adaptable that they could

**Zeppelin showing
their metal mettle**

try out so many different styles and play them with such consummate professionalism. Bonham plays some titanic breaks as the band gets stuck into a swing groove. The overall mood recalls Queen's 'Crazy Little Thing Called Love' and doubtless owes much to the same sources of inspiration.

Lyrically speaking, Plant is excited by the spectacle of one of his many mythical loves. She is wearing such a tight dress, he is inspired to call out "Come on baby, give me some". Naturally enough, the dress also arouses the familiar passion of jealousy and he quite clearly explains that, "When I see you walking with all those guys, it makes me feel so sick". This is just the sort of situation that leads to violence in many public bars and dance halls. The number eventually transmogrifies itself into an unexpected jam session with a long fade out. Freddie Mercury – eat your heart out.

When it came to apportioning tracks on the original album, 'Darlene' would have been a much better bet than 'South Bound Saurez'.

BONZO'S MONTREAUX

The Mighty Bonzo shows that the drums can be a musical instrument. Far removed from the tearaway stuff of 'Moby Dick', this is the drummer in thoughtful, constructive mode. He creates a tune on the drums, aided by electronically-processed tymps, tom toms and that famous Ludwig snare drum that was usually at the heart of the matter. Dubbed the John Bonham Drum Orchestra, this was Bonham embarking on a percussion adventure that was devised with the aid of Page, who added electronic treatments, which included the use of a Harmonizer. It was recorded on September 12, 1976, at Mountain Studios, Montreaux, the Swiss town on the edge of Lake Geneva that remains home to one of the world's best annual music festivals and is a popular haunt for visiting rock musicians.

Divided into sections, the piece rumbles along at a leisurely pace, sounding not unlike a steel band about

to fall down an escalator. Many found these rhythmic electronics harsh on the ears when first unveiled in 1982. 'Moby Dick' and 'Bonzo's Montreaux' were slotted together on the re-mastered six-LP boxed set *Led Zeppelin* (Atlantic 7567 – 82144-1) released in 1990.

Although Bonham was a master drummer, he had a realistic attitude to the role of the drummer in rock. "Not everybody likes or understands a drum solo, so I like to bring in effects and sounds to keep their interest," he explained. "I used to play a hand drum solo long before I joined Zeppelin. I played a solo on the Duke Ellington tune 'Caravan' when I was only 16. Sometimes I'd take a chunk out of my knuckles on the hi-hat, or catch my hand on the tension rods. With Zeppelin I tried to play something different every night in my solos. I'd play for 20 minutes but the longest ever was 30 minutes. It's a long time, but when I was playing it seemed to fly by. Sometimes you'd come up against a brick wall and you'd think: 'How am I going to get out of this one?' Or sometimes you go into a fill and you'd know halfway through it was going to be disastrous. There were times when I blundered and got the dreaded look from the lads. But that was a good sign. It showed I'd attempted something I'd not tried before."

WEARING AND TEARING

I

t starts out like a murmur then it grows like thunder", warns Plant. A fast jam from Polar Studios, cut on November 21, 1978, this is a splendid rave-up from a band who were already disappearing into the mists by the time *Coda* was released. It's a real headbanger, and a reminder that despite 'Ozone Baby' and 'All My Love', Led Zeppelin were still capable of rocking out – right to the end of their days. Plant's lyrics are mostly indecipherable, but you can hear him sing what sounds like: "I'm going to ask for medication... who cares for

"Woarrgh!" Bonham drops a bass drum on his foot

medication when you're falling apart?" He later adds, "What's that creeping up behind you? It's just an old friend". The guitars blast back in response and suddenly the whole band shuts down, leaving a faint trace echo, like the final shudder of an earthquake.

Page and Plant had said this was the number that would knock the young punk bands off their high horse, and was planned as a single for release in time for their 1979 Knebworth shows. However, it missed the deadline because of problems with the pressing. Robert Plant later said that they wanted to put the record out on a different label under the name of a phoney band to compete with The Damned and the Sex Pistols. "It was so vicious and so fresh," recalled Robert. It certainly would have been fun to confuse the critics and their perceived rivals and it would have shown that the members of Led Zeppelin were still young, fresh and just as virile as the opposition. It was presumably intended for inclusion on *In Through The Out Door*. In the event, it was never aired in public until Page and Plant performed it together at the Knebworth Festival in 1990.

> **" NOT EVERYBODY LIKES OR UNDERSTANDS A DRUM SOLO, SO I LIKE TO BRING IN EFFECTS AND SOUNDS TO KEEP THEIR INTEREST. "**
>
> JOHN BONHAM

**Overleaf:
The Power & The
Glory**

10 REMASTERS & UNLEDDED

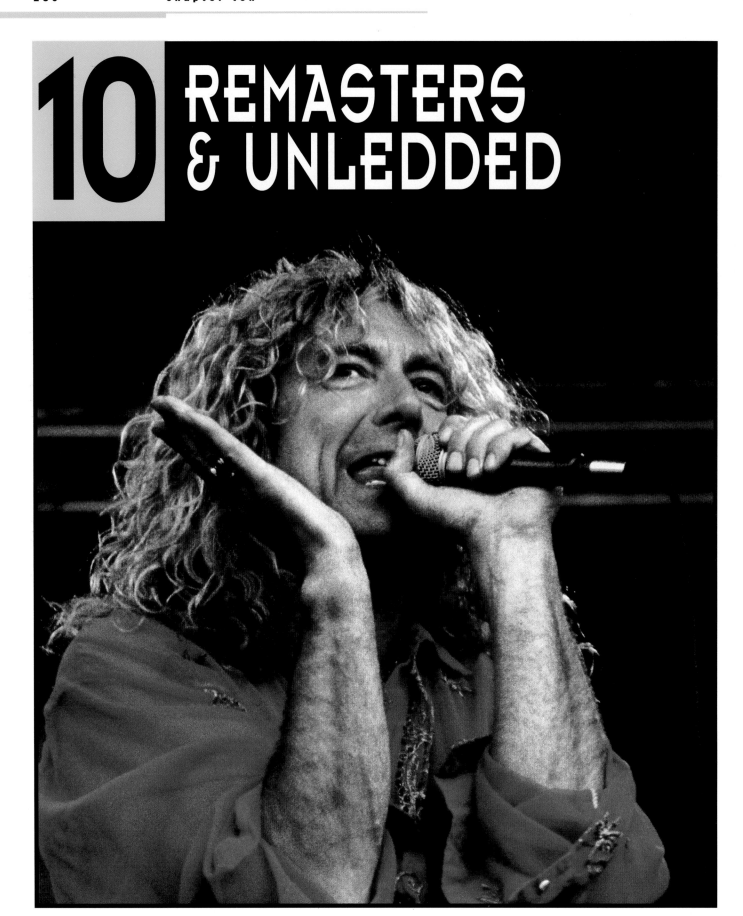

In 1990 Jimmy Page set about the task of remastering the classic Led Zeppelin original recordings. During the 80s Atlantic Records had made the Zeppelin catalogue of albums available on compact disc for the first time, but quality was lost during the transfer and Page was unhappy with the results. Many of the subtle aspects of the music had been lost – there was a lot of tape hiss, and vocals and guitars seemed to suffer badly in the mixes, when heard on CD. Page set to work to remaster the material from the original tapes, for release in a special boxed set. Digital remastering began with the assistance of George Marino at Sterling Sound, New York and was completed in one week in May 1990. The results were brilliant and for those who owned scratchy 70s copies of vinyl LPs, the sounds were a revelation. It was like seeing a famous painting restored, with the years of grime wiped away. On October 15, 1990, a triple album and double CD/Cassette of Zeppelin material – called simply *Remasters* – was released in the UK and Europe. This was the condensed version of the 54 track monster boxed-set of six LPs called *Led Zeppelin* released in the US on October 23, 1990 and world-wide on October 29, 1990. It came complete with previously unreleased tracks and an illustrated booklet containing informative essays. This was hotly pursued by another compilation *Led Zeppelin Boxed Set 2*, released in 1993, comprising two CDs with all 31 tracks from the band's nine studio albums, not included on the 1990 Boxed Set, plus one previously unreleased track. The boxed sets were a big success despite the high price (£50) they commanded, and sold over a million units in a couple of years. They were an artistic success as well – Zeppelin's work had not really been fully appreciated by contemporary critics and the re-issue of so much classic material helped many to understand just how important and influential the band had been. The *Led Zeppelin* set came in a deluxe box, with a brilliantly conceived cover design, showing a series of crop circles with the shadow of a Zeppelin airship hovering overhead. John Paul Jones and Robert Plant were called in to give their official blessing to the project and the choice of tracks. While they weren't presented in strict chronological order, the odd juxtaposition of songs from different eras served to underline the huge range of material the band covered, while maintaining an outstanding musical consistency. Spoilt for choice, fans were then presented with all the Led Zeppelin studio albums which were reissued, in re-mastered editions, in 1993's Atlantic boxed set *Led Zeppelin – The Complete Studio Recordings*.

LED ZEPPELIN
(ATLANTIC 7567-82144-1) 1990

Among the fifty-four tracks on the six LP boxed set, there were four items previously unreleased in album format.

TRAVELLING RIVERSIDE BLUES

What could be described as a fairly routine blues number is transformed by some wonderful slide guitar work by Jimmy Page and cheeky, exuberant and muscular vocals from young Master Plant. "Squeeze my lemon until the juice runs down my leg", exhorts Plant, imbuing the time-honoured Robert Johnson phrase with new vigour. It's great to hear Zeppelin in the period when they were still an up-and-coming British blues band, long before they were elevated into the stadium rock-peerage. This track was originally recorded for DJ John Peel's *Top Gear* BBC radio show, on June 24, 1969, and has all the clean, efficient recording quality you'd expect from radio. No tricks or surprises, but the band is in tune, and you can hear all the instruments – it was a shame BBC engineers at the Maida Vale studios didn't work on producing rock albums in the 60s. The track was recorded live in the studio without an audience, but there was no lack of atmosphere and Page was able to add some overdubs, including an excellent solo. He decided to add it to the boxed set because he had so many requests for information about the number during his US *Outrider* tour in 1988. The track itself

Left:

Robert Plant –

Re-Master Of

The Universe

had been released on a promo CD single and was played so frequently on US radio it became a *Billboard Rock Tracks* hit in November 1990. The song is credited to Plant, Page and Robert Johnson, who came up with the original lines back in 1937. Robert Plant was particularly enamoured with the free-wheeling, sexual spirit of the song, with its folk and blues roots. This performance, dubbed 'Travelling Riverside Blues 69', was produced by John Walters and broadcast on June 28, 1969. BBC Enterprises subsequently gave Page the go-ahead to include it on the boxed set.

Blues, sweat and beers – the 60s!

HEY HEY WHAT CAN I DO

 relic of the *Led Zeppelin III* era, and written at Bron-y-Aur cottage, this was originally only available on a UK Atlantic Records sampler album called *The New Age Of Atlantic*. Released in 1972, it sold for the

princely sum of 99p. A jolly piece filled with strumming mandolins and acoustic guitars, Plant turns to the world for help as he announces: "Hey, hey, what can I do? I've got a little woman but she won't be true." A frequent problem but not one that causes the singer more than passing heartache. After all – he can always drink his sorrows away. Plant is nicely restrained on a poppy song which requires him to sing in a lower key than usual with far less shouting. This group composition has a theme redolent of the West Coast and could be called a hippy's lament. It fades out in some chaos, which might suggest it was a trial run for a song weeded out of the final album-selection process. Yet according to Peter Grant the song was actually intended to be a single. Recorded at Island Studios in 1970, and engineered by Andy Johns, it was featured on the B-side of the US single 'Immigrant Song', released on November 5, 1970. The song was revived and performed on the Plant/Page world tour of 1995.

format to allow them to play more music. *In Concert* was a one-hour show and became a long running institution. Jimmy Page has pointed out that although the track was cut live, the respectful audience sat in silent enjoyment. His extended performance here is worth the price of the boxed set alone – there is something rather touching about what is, in effect, a musical recital, stripped of screaming fans shouting "Jimmy!" Everything else fades into the background, while the young guitar player becomes as one with his instrument – his subtle use of harmonics is remarkable. John Bonham carefully adds a little percussive support, but it's Jimmy Page playing acoustically, with greater fluidity and more space than he does on any studio albums, that remains the focal point. The guitar's constant changes of tempo, volume and tone creates a hypnotic effect that clearly entrances the audience. Sheer music triumphs over all and says more than a thousand screams – or a thousand words.

A debonair Page relaxing at his Thameside Boathouse home in 1970

WHITE SUMMER/ BLACK MOUNTAIN SIDE

 superb demonstration of Page's acoustic guitar skills, this was recorded and broadcast live on June 27, 1969 at the Playhouse Theatre, London for a Radio One show produced by Jeff Griffin. The previously unreleased cut was included on the album by arrangement with the BBC. Intended as a pilot for Radio One's *In Concert* series, it came about as a result of Page enjoying the previous BBC broadcast for *Top Gear* and asking if it was possible to expand the

MOBY DICK/ BONZO'S MONTREAUX

clever blending of two John Bonham showcase numbers produces a fitting tribute to the great drummer. Both tracks ran at the same tempo so Page was able to put the two together; he used a metronome to check them out and a Synclavier at Atlantic's New York facilities to merge the two. 'Moby Dick' was originally recorded in 1969 at Mirror Sound, Los Angeles and at Mayfair Studios, New York and was mixed at A&R Studios, New York with Eddie Kramer. It was released on *Led Zeppelin II* in 1969. 'Bonzo's Montreaux' was recorded on December 12, 1976 at Mountain Studios, Montreaux, Switzerland and engineered by John Timperly. The two cuts received the most internal votes from the band and Page didn't want to leave either one off the album; in fact he discards Bonham's original 'Moby Dick' snare drum and tom tom work which was rather slow to take off. After the familiar heavy guitar theme, the piece cuts straight to the more dynamic 'Bonzo's Montreaux', with its electronic treatments. It all makes for a much more satisfying percussion outing that is structured, melodic and adventurous. It's just a shame that nobody recorded Bonham's snare drum solo at Carnegie Hall in 1969, or any of his other more orthodox drum work-outs.

LED ZEPPELIN BOXED SET 2

BABY COME ON HOME

hat they used to call a slow rock-a-ballad in the heyday of 60s soul, this is very much a tribute to the kind of music Plant loved and the sort of records Page and Jones might have played on during their session days in the 60s. The only previously unreleased cut on the second boxed set, it shows a completely different side to Led Zeppelin. Apart from the cascading drum fills, which are unmistakably Bonham, this could be the genuine article from Detroit City. Plant gets down on his knees in supplication, while Jones and Page provide suitably sanctified gospel-style organ and guitar. Recorded at Olympic Studios, London, this curiosity was rescued from oblivion when a reel of tape was found marked 'Yardbirds, October 10, 1968'. The tape vanished for many years, but eventually turned up in a dustbin outside the studio in 1991. The piece was ironically marked by the engineer 'Tribute To Bert Berns' who was the American composer of such hits as 'Hang On Sloopy', and producer of Van Morrison. It was later salvaged by Mike Fraser, who co-produced the Coverdale/Page album, and restored to its former glory.

NO QUARTER
(Fontana 526 362-2) 1994

s 1993 dawned Plant was busy with his *Fate Of Nations* album and Jimmy Page was shacked up with David 'Whitesnake' Coverdale, but the Led Zeppelin reunion rumours just wouldn't go away, fuelled by insider gossip from people who actually knew what was going on. There had been so much speculation and so many repeated denials that it seemed that never the twain should meet. Yet when Plant arrived in Boston, Massachusetts, in November, 1993, for one of his own shows at the Orpheum, Page dropped by to see Plant's band, say hello and wish him luck. Jimmy Page was officially on his way to Los Angeles to rehearse with David Coverdale, for a trip to Japan, but there was a much more exciting idea hanging in the air. Plant had recently been invited by MTV to record an *Unplugged* show and suddenly it dawned on them that they could combine forces in a way that wouldn't just be a Zeppelin reunion. They could write some new material together, try different things and refashion a few of the old classics that meant most to them. Plant was particularly excited about a CD he'd heard featuring Moroccan singer, Najat Aatabou; it was inspirational and it plugged into their affinities with the desert and the music of the Middle East. Page and Plant was born – and it was good.

Events then moved at speed – the Coverdale project was hastily concluded and swiftly forgotten. The old mates went off to Marrakech to record some Moroccan-style material in a local market place, in front of a crowd of bemused and excited onlookers, then they went on a nostalgic trip to Wales, near the scene of their 1970's trip to Bron-y-Aur cottage. Location filming went ahead for the proposed MTV special, then Plant and Page returned to London to begin rehearsing new numbers, with part of Plant's band, which consisted of his son-in-law Charlie Jones (bass) and exciting young drummer, Michael Lee, formerly with the Little Angels and The Cult. They brought in guitarist Porl Thompson, from The Cure, and put together an eight-piece Egyptian orchestra, made up of percussion and string players from London and Cairo. The MTV show was recorded at London Weekend TV studios and, after transmission, was made available on a ninety-minute Warner Music Vision video *No Quarter – Unledded* (1995). Among the musicians appearing on the show were Najma Akhtar (vocals), Jim Sutherland (mandolin and bodhran), Nigel Eaton (hurdy gurdy), Ed Shearmur (Hammond organ), and Hossam Ramzy (doholla and musical director). Also incorporated were the London Metropolitan Orchestra and the Egyptian Ensemble, and together they made an extraordinary sound. It wasn't Led Zeppelin but it was a major step forward for two catalytic personalities, who only needed each other's presence to create credible music and an incredible atmosphere.

One person was missing from this unexpected reunion – although John Paul Jones had appeared with Plant and Page on the occasional Led Zep reunion, he wasn't invited to take part in the new project, apparently to avoid too many comparisons with the old band. John Paul Jones had tended to keep a rather low profile during the post-Zeppelin years and had spent much of his time in his Devonshire home, keeping out of the public's eye. However, in 1984 he worked with film director, Michael Winner, on the music for Winner's movie *Scream For Help*. The soundtrack album was released on Atlantic in April, 1985. On one of the

Robert and Jimmy face the press during the launch of 'No Quarter'

tracks, 'When You Fall In Love,' Jones took the lead vocals. Jones also appeared in the Paul McCartney movie *Give My Regards to Broad Street* and contributed three tracks to a Ben E. King album called *Save The Last Dance For Me* (1987). More significantly, he encouraged Wayne Hussey's band The Mission, which was heavily influenced by Led Zeppelin. Jones had been sent the band's demo and then offered to become their producer on an album called *Children*, on which he played keyboards. He joined Page, Plant and Jason Bonham for the Atlantic Records Fortieth Anniversary concert, and for more recent awards ceremonies, but remained the least visible of the Zeppelin line-up.

For all those who had waited to see them reunited so long, the next step for Page and Plant was even bolder and more unbelievable than the MTV show. The duo were planning to set off on a complete world tour that would last an entire year. With the organisational help of Plant's manager Bill Curbishley, they could celebrate their past and create a real future – it was a dream time. The tour began at the Pensacola Civic Centre, Florida, on Sunday, February 26, 1995 and went on to criss-cross North America until the following May. During April they visited Boston, the city where Led Zeppelin first played in the US, way back in 1968, and where the new Plant-Page union was first conceived. Playing to a crowd of twenty thousand, this kind of attention was more like the old days. They played mostly Led Zeppelin material including such favourites as 'Thank You', 'Wanton Song', 'Bring it On Home', 'Ramble On', 'No Quarter', 'Gallows Pole', 'When The Levee Breaks', 'Four Sticks' and a massive version of 'Kashmir'. One number was missing from the set list – 'Stairway To Heaven' was dismissed by Plant as redundant, although Page couldn't resist occasionally playing a few teasing bars. As the tour rumbled on, the band added such numbers as 'Rock And Roll', 'That's The Way', 'Heartbreaker' and 'Babe I'm Gonna Leave You'. Plant and Page remained on good terms throughout the epic journey although Plant occasionally referred to themselves as the Jack Lemmon and Walter Matthau of rock'n'roll. It was a particularly auspicious home-coming when Page and Plant played at Madison Square Garden, New York on October 26 and 27, 1995. They were greeted as long-lost friends and went down a storm as they encored with 'Black Dog' and 'Kashmir'. At the end of the evening Plant greeted the crowds with the oblique remark of "See you again when we have some new ideas."

While taking in dates in Mexico, South America and Japan, the tour also visited Europe in June and they included shows in France, Holland, Belgium, and Germany. They returned to England for an appearance at Glastonbury Festival, England on June 25, 1995. During the tour the band gradually played with less emphasis on the Egyptian effects and the songs returned to their more familiar rock setting. A total of thirty-two classic songs from the Zeppelin catalogue were played on various shows during the Plant-Page tour including 'Achilles Last Stand', 'Babe I'm Gonna Leave You', 'Black Dog', 'Bring It On Home', 'Celebration Day', 'Dancing Days', 'Four Sticks', 'Friends', 'Gallows Pole', 'Goin' To California', 'Good Times Bad Times', 'Heartbreaker', 'Hey Hey What Can I Do', 'I Can't Quit You', 'In The Evening', 'Kashmir', 'No Quarter', 'Nobody's Fault But Mine', 'Over The Hills And Far Away', 'Rainsong', 'Ramble On', 'Rock And Roll', 'Since I've Been Loving You', 'Tangerine', 'Thank You', 'That's The Way', 'The Battle Of Evermore', 'The Song Remains The Same', 'Wanton Song', 'What Is And What Should Never Be', 'When The Levee Breaks', and 'Whole Lotta Love'. Fans were entranced as these were all numbers that they never expected to hear played live again. The duo, and their entourage, went on to play several other major UK gigs including Sheffield Arena (July 13), Cornwall Coliseum (15), Birmingham NEC (22, 23), and London's Wembley Arena (25 and 26). They also managed to fit in a few low-key events at smaller capacity two-thousand-seater venues, rather in the spirit of their small club tour of the early 70s. By the end of the tour in Melbourne, Australia, in March, 1996, Plant, Page and their entourage had played some one hundred and fifteen shows in nineteen countries during three hundred and seventy days of solid work.

Tracks on the Plant/Page *No Quarter* CD included a smaller selection of songs from the MTV show than were included on the video. 'Nobody's Fault But Mine', 'Thank You', 'No Quarter', 'Friends', 'Yallah', 'City Don't Cry', 'Since I've Been Loving You', The Battle Of Evermore', 'Wonderful One', 'Wah Wah', 'That's The Way', 'Gallows Pole', 'Four Sticks', and 'Kashmir', gave a fascinating taste of past triumphs mixed with contemporary world-music concepts. Certainly 'Gallows Pole' benefited from their updated treatment and 'Kashmir' took on a whole new and, somewhat, mystical light in their East-meets-West approach.

YALLAH

ould this have been the way ahead if Led Zeppelin had survived after 1980, or were these desert songs just a riddle in the sands of time? On the *Unledded* video, 'Yallah' (also known as 'The Truth Explodes') featured Page and Plant performing to a backing tape of heavy Eastern drums in the crowded market place in Marrakech. Page uses the electronic Theramin during this hypnotic and strangely funky performance. As an electric guitar riff grinds behind him, Plant throws back his head to emit a cry of "Ah ah – oh oh", which seems to express the inner yearnings of the wandering Nomad cut off from humanity; despite his loneliness, he is still assailed by the same temptations that face all Mankind. Such simple vocal techniques can be heard used among the inhabitants of central Asia, from the deserts to the mountains. These wailing tones have a timeless quality that stretches back to the days of the great caravans and, even, Biblical times. 'Yallah' was played live on the Plant-Page tour for the first time at Corestates Spectrum, Philadelphia on Tuesday April 4, 1995 when it replaced 'Calling You', a song from Plant's *Fate Of Nations* album, in the band's set list.

CITY DON'T CRY

h City, don't cry!" implores Plant, "City don't weep." This is a call for peace, understanding and sympathy, set to a lilting melody. Situated in west-central Morocco, near the Atlas mountains, the city of Marrakech, with its population of 1,517,000, has extensive gardens and a fourteenth-century palace, while the minaret of the Koutoubya mosque dominates the skyline. This city was the historic setting for this attractive vignette on which Page plays understated acoustic guitar while Plant claps his hands and sings with quavering passion. This simple theme was filmed in a courtyard in Marrakech, with three Egyptian musicians playing traditional instruments, including hand drums and bongos which give a gentle rhythmic impetus.

WONDERFUL ONE

his track was recorded live in the London TV studios, with Page sitting on a large wood chair, playing a double-neck guitar, while Plant sings a doleful melody and poetic lyrics with touching sincerity. The lyrics address women with rather more respect than is usual in blues-shouting circles. Plant seems to be addressing a desert maiden with her yashmak on, from a safe distance "Who must lie beside the thief – whose golden tongue will she believe?" he asks. "Touch me with fire, my mind is undone – my freedom has come. I trip through desire my wonderful one." Here is a song that celebrates the joys of male and female bonding, Eastern style, and may have lessons for those engaged in the rather more debased courting habits prevalent in Western society. This was one of the tracks that intrigued Plant and Page sufficiently to go back into the studio and start performing new material together again.

WAH WAH

lso recorded and filmed in the court yard in Marrakech, bongos and drums are to the fore as Plant sings "Give me peace of mind and bury all my pain and years of being sad." The chorus of "Wah wah" interrupts this reverie until Plant reiterates his plea to Allah to "bury all the pain beneath the sand." The piece begins to accelerate towards a dignified crescendo and, despite the apparent monotony of much middle-eastern music, it is possible to identify the links with Western folk song and even Scottish bagpipes, which utilize the drone to such searing effect. Led Zeppelin began with the blues and spread out to embrace the music of the world, but their roots remain the same. After all, in the final analysis, "Wah Wah" is not so far removed in spirit from "Baby, baby".

Overleaf:
Plant and Page, the
old firm back again

11 THE LONG FAREWELL
1980-1994

Jimmy Page and Robert Plant were like nomads wandering in the desert, after the demise of Led Zeppelin. Exhausted and thirsty, they paused at the oasis of each new solo musical endeavour, hoping to find sustenance. Driven apart by the stresses and strains of the old group's latter days, they could not work together, but despite their best efforts, they could not work apart. There was no more poignant sight than Jimmy Page playing 'Stairway To Heaven' alone on stage at The Royal Albert Hall, in 1983. For his part, Robert Plant in solo mode could never command the huge audiences he had once enjoyed with Zeppelin. Pride kept the two apart, yet hell had no fury greater than Plant's when Page finally settled for working with other singers in the absence of his old partner. In fact over a decade passed before the pair were re-united in a project that was relevant, fruitful and satisfying to both themselves and their eager audience.

For years they were assailed by an unending clamour for "a Led Zeppelin reunion", yet even their greatest fans feared the consequences if it was tried and went wrong. Nobody wanted to see such an event destroy the memory of the much loved and respected band. Whenever they did give way to the pressure, the results seemed to bear out the fans' worst fears; two public attempts at a reunion produced plenty of nostalgia but nothing that resembled the power of the old band. Behind the scenes, rehearsals with a revamped Zeppelin came to nothing. All along it was Plant who, understandably, seemed least keen on going back. While the public remembered a wildly successful and hugely influential rock band, he remembered all too well the negative aspects of Zeppelin's latter days. In 1980 he was still young and had the chance to create a working environment and take charge of his own destiny. At long last he could call the shots, and sing and play the music he wanted to do, perhaps in a more modern, contemporary style.

Plant described the end of Zeppelin in dramatic terms: "It was like staggering away from the vacuum caused by a great explosion, with your eardrums ringing. I found myself standing on a street corner, clutching twelve years of my life, with a lump in my throat and a tear in my eye, and not knowing which way to go. It was a most peculiar experience, because I knew that the dream was over and everything had gone. It was just a memory."

Both Plant and Page suffered deeply from the catastrophic end of what had been their whole way of life, and they responded and learned to deal with the situation in broadly similar ways. Plant had been cut off from the mainstream of musical activity by his ten-year commitment to Zeppelin and Jimmy Page. Suddenly he found himself alone and had to set about finding the right musicians to help create a new band. "With Zeppelin it was so comfortable that I never had a thought beyond our records and tours. Socially it might have been better for me to have met more people."

One thing was sure, when John Bonham died Plant was convinced that Led Zeppelin was finished and there was no point in trying to carry on with a replacement drummer. In the immediate aftermath of the tragedy he locked himself away and spent several months virtually in hiding. Eventually he began to come out to visit local clubs, watched bands play, met musicians and finally began to assemble his own group called The Honeydrippers. They even went out to play low-key gigs, without billing their celebrated singer. It was the same sort of tactics adopted by Paul McCartney when he was creating Wings in the aftermath of The Beatles. Plant found the exercise good therapy as he worked out his musical game plan. "The Honeydrippers got me at it again. It was great fun to be able to go out and play without any of the usual pressures," he recalled. The band's line up included Robbie Blunt (guitar), Andy Sylvester (bass), Kevin O'Neil (drums) and a brace of sax players, and they made their debut in Stourbridge on March 9, 1981. There was hardly any publicity and few outside the area even knew the band existed. "It was an exercise for me to regain confidence and find out if I could still sing. I wanted to get back in front of people, face to face."

The band played mainly blues and r&b covers, and went down a storm at their first few gigs. Then

> **" I FOUND MYSELF STANDING ON A STREET CORNER, CLUTCHING TWELVE YEARS OF MY LIFE, WITH A LUMP IN MY THROAT AND A TEAR IN MY EYE, AND NOT KNOWING WHICH WAY TO GO. "**
>
> ROBERT PLANT

Left:
Plant, Page and
Egyptian orchestra,
recording the
***Unledded* TV special**

problems arose when the band members, naturally enough, began to wonder why they couldn't play bigger venues and earn some money. They wanted a shot at the big time, after all their lead singer was internationally famous and they should be able to command more than the price of a cheese sandwich and a packet of cigarettes. Plant wanted to keep to the small club circuit but was beginning to tire of playing the same old standards; he'd done all that before as a teenager. Now he needed some new material and began writing songs in odd moments with the band's guitarist, Robbie Blunt.

Said Plant: "I had fun with the Honeydrippers and enjoyed myself tremendously, but felt it was high time to do some original material. We began to realize the limitations as things got repetitious, so between gigs we started sitting down at a four-track tape machine and writing." Blunt and Plant began working on Plant's long awaited solo album, which was recorded at Rockfield Studios in Wales. Among those playing on the session were Cozy Powell (drums), Paul Martinez (bass) and Jess Woodroffe (keyboards); Phil Collins also sat in on some of the sessions when Powell was busy elsewhere. It wasn't all plain sailing – although Plant had known Blunt for some years he found it very traumatic working with someone other than Jimmy Page. If they'd found a song that really worked, he and Page would work into the small hours, whereas his new partners got tired after a couple of hours in the studio. Furthermore, some of the older hands weren't afraid to give Plant advice – when the singer tried to be cool and laid back in the studio Cozy Powell shouted: "Go on, do all of that screaming!"

Plant later admitted that he went back to see his old mate for advice during this testing period. "When I was recording the album I kept taking tapes over to Jimmy to get his opinion. It was very emotional. Like there were times when I just wanted to cry and hold his hand. When I played Jimmy the complete album he knew then that I had gone, and I was forging ahead alone."

The new-look Plant created a good impression when he finally launched his solo career. *Pictures At Eleven*, his debut solo album and first studio work in three years, was released in June 1982. The critics were kind, new listeners were prepared to give it a hearing, and old fans gave it a qualified vote of approval. It wasn't quite what they'd been hoping for, but then

Plant couldn't start afresh by singing 'Whole Lotta Love – Part II'. *Pictures* was the start of a series of sometimes rather serious, elliptical albums like *The Principle Of Moments* (1983) and *Shaken'n'Stirred* (1985), lightened up by the inclusion of his bluesy ten-inch LP *The Honeydrippers Volume 1* (1984). During 1983 Plant broke up with his wife Maureen, and moved from the farm in the Midlands he'd bought in Zeppelin days, to live in London and be at the centre of the music business. He joked about life on his old ten-acre farm. "I had two dogs, six goats, several ducks and a beer belly. All have gone now."

His records sold well, and he had a hit with 'Big Log', a single from *The Principle Of Moments*, but while the first album went Gold, it didn't do as well as *Coda*, which sold a million copies worldwide. In 1988 he formed a new band and released *Now & Zen*, his most satisfying work in some time, which yielded the singles 'Heaven Knows', the exciting 'Tall Cool One', and 'Ship Of Fools.' Perhaps stung by the success of Whitesnake (fronted by David Coverdale), Plant returned to his rock roots on an album that included several Zeppelin samples and even had Jimmy Page guesting on one track. It seemed to signal that Plant had at last come to terms with his past. In 1990 he released another album *Manic Nirvana*, written and recorded during the previous year. His band at this time included Chris Blackwell (drums), Doug Boyle (guitars), Phil Johnstone (keyboards) and Charlie Jones (bass). In his tour programme that year Plant wrote: "Success is fleeting, obscurity's forever. Good luck, see you on the pile!"

After three solo albums and his ten-inch *Honeydrippers* set which sold two million copies in the States (more than *The Principle Of Moments*) Plant felt that his audience had become confused about his musical direction. "Some people lost the plot and the momentum changed and got distorted. I kept trucking along, pursuing this kind of aim to create an alternative brand of music that borrows from Led Zeppelin but is primarily me. People I was working with kept saying 'Let's go back and do this,' and I'd say 'No, you have to stop and take stock and write material that has more energy.'" Plant agreed that some of his post-Zeppelin work had become rather austere. "I was probably going up my own arse a bit in trying to be different, and trying to keep away from the mainstream. I thought I had

Left:
Robert Plant with
guitarist Robbie Blunt

A new hair do, a new future

better get back in there now 'cos I like the glory y'know." Plant was angry that David Coverdale (with flowing blonde hair) was enjoying chart success with an act that seemed to be based on Plant's image as the sexy blonde blues man. Coverdale himself later conceded with a smile that this had been "a hairdressing error."

But if Whitesnake was hard to take, there was even more outrage to come when German singer Lenny Wolf created a complete Zeppelin-style band, called Kingdom Come, featuring guitarist Danny Stag, which played astoundingly accurate impersonations of the Zeppelin sound. Instead of being rejected by outraged fans, it was actually welcomed by a younger audience, probably unfamiliar with the twenty-year-old original albums that served as a role model. The technically perfect Kingdom Come album was a hit in America, only a month after the release of *Now And Zen*. Rock music hates a vacuum, but some stalwart British rock musicians rushed to defend the elder statesmen. Gary Moore on his 1988 album *After The*

War featured a song which accused Kingdom Come of being 'Led Clones'. The upstart band was short-lived and broke up in 1989. However, they had proved that there was a deep hunger for the kind of rock music that only Led Zeppelin could provide and if the originators wouldn't get back together, then the fans would get their music elsewhere.

Three years later *Fate Of Nations*, Plant's 1993 offering, came hot on the heels of the *Coverdale Page* album, the fruit of an unexpected collaboration between David Coverdale and the old master. By now Plant was in his mid-forties and moving into a more mature vocal style, but the choice of material wasn't especially in tune with the expectations of rock fans, who had by then turned to such bands as Guns'n'Roses and grunge alternatives like Nirvana and Pearl Jam. Plant was still very proud of his past but continued to keep his distance from a Led Zeppelin reunion. On *Fate Of Nations* he worked with producer Chris Hughes and was energized by Phonogram's A&R man, Dave Bates, who signed him to Fontana. Plant's new music was mainly recorded live in the studio, using such musicians as Charlie Jones and Phil Johnstone, with Kevin Scott MacMichael on guitars. There were also guest appearances by artists like Richard Thompson and violinist Nigel Kennedy, who appeared on an Arabic-type track called 'Calling You'. Talking about his approach to the album Plant commented:

"I made a conscious approach to get away from all the isms and computer technology, all the self-conscious awareness of what's current and fashionable. I've always been neurotic about my voice. I remember getting all those awards in the early 70s and being voted Top Male Vocalist in the polls. I look at the awards now and think – 'How did I ever do that!' At the time, with Led Zeppelin, I used to say 'Keep the voice down in the mix – keep it quiet.' With Zeppelin, part of the atmosphere was to get the voice woven into the instruments. The music on my *Fate Of Nations* album was probably as near organically in construction and thought process as I will ever get to 'Ramble On' and stuff like that. Consciously and intentionally that's been my plan. Whether it's commercially viable or not I always have to be 100 per cent obsessed with what I'm doing. I have learnt to be more patient in the studio and learnt not to say 'That's great, that'll do okay.' I did a lot of vocals over the years that probably could

Plant – calling you!

have been improved upon, although I've always had a reputation as being a distinctive vocalist and there have been a lot of people who have used my style as their style. I've always believed that what counts most of all is that the delivery is natural and impromptu. I couldn't imagine Howlin' Wolf dropping in line three on 'Smokestack Lightning', know what I mean?"

At this stage in his career, Plant found it quite an experience working with people who were ready to give their ideas and give him a firm sense of direction. "I'm grateful for having an A&R man like David Bates. Hellfire! Does he teach you how to suck eggs – Jesus Christ! I had to learn a lot of restraint on my own personality. I'm quite a volatile character y'know, and I've learnt that I'm not the only one who knows what's right, even though it's me singing and me writing the lyrics. It's been very interesting and I've enjoyed it. I like to try new things and see how they fit me. As a singer there's no point in keeping the same persona forever and ever. You have to do things for yourself, not what everybody expects. I could not have kept the old line, like some 60s singers who eke out a living by treading the same old path. I don't know whether they cry at night or roll over in bed scratching their fat bellies and say 'Hey, that's another farewell tour we pulled off.' I've been to some of these reconstructions of youth and they don't really stick. I mean rock'n'roll was always supposed to be something that came from the mind, heart and loins. You can't work with the same people forever and say: 'Hey, this is youth music!'"

In 1993, a year before the Plant/Page reunion, Plant was still resisting all attempts at recreating Led Zeppelin as a commercial proposition. "Led Zeppelin came out of the underground scene. It was all a clannish thing. But people's vitality for music changes once they reach a certain age. It dulls off, so a lot of people who were into Zep have grown out of their denim jackets and they're listening to Chris Rea. Makes you weep to think about it! There are a lot of people jumping onto bandwagons. Some people just do it for the money. People say to me 'You could really make a killing here.' And I say, 'Oh yeah, how would I do that?' Ha, ha! You see before Zep, Jimmy Page was in groups and I was in groups and after Zep, we went into different groups again. I love what we did together. Some of it was superb. I also remember some of the conditions it was created in, some of it

not so good. But none of that matters now because Led Zeppelin is now a timepiece. You have to move on in every respect."

Jimmy Page had to move on too after the demise of Led Zeppelin, but for the man who had created the band, it was difficult to entirely shake off his roots. He was, after all, the personification of Zeppelin, a rock vision, burned into everyone's mind. The curly-haired guitarist, violin bow aloft, eyes shut in ecstasy, creating the eerie sound of 'Dazed And Confused', or duck walking across the stage to 'Rock And Roll' – this was an image that was hard to abandon or replace. Shattered mentally and physically by the stress and strain of the last five years, Page, like Plant, withdrew from the scene for the first years of the 80s. John Paul Jones explained the background circumstances to their collective withdrawal from the scene: "When Bonzo died we had actually been rehearsing for the American tour and there was a lot of optimism. The band was in good form but it just had to stop. The music needed those particular four people to make it work. We could have had another band with another drummer, but it wouldn't have been Zeppelin. That died with John."

Jimmy Page was so distraught by Bonham's death that it seemed he might never play the guitar again. Virtually overnight he had lost the part of his life that was devoted to touring, recording and making music with Led Zeppelin. Eventually, however, he plucked up courage and began to play at the odd jam sessions. He bought Sol Studios in Cookham, Berkshire, from producer Gus Dudgeon, and spent most of his time there working on various projects, with supportive visitors like Elton John and George Harrison. But he remained a recluse as far as the outside world was concerned.

Then on March 10, 1981 he sat in with Jeff Beck at the Odeon Hammersmith, London, and made a guest appearance that delighted the audience. Plant, Jones and Page also met up at a charity show at the Golden Lion pub in Fulham. Page finally returned to the studios, not to launch a new band, but to write and

> **" WHETHER IT'S COMMERCIALLY VIABLE OR NOT I ALWAYS HAVE TO BE 100 PER CENT OBSESSED WITH WHAT I'M DOING. "**
>
> ROBERT PLANT

Left:

James Patrick Page –

musician

Page at Cambridge Folk Festival 1984 with Tony Franklin (centre) and Roy Harper (right)

record the music for a new Michael Winner film *Death Wish 2*, which yielded a soundtrack album. It was taking Page much longer than it had taken Plant to make a full return to public performances, but he needed a respite from the music business which had been his major preoccupation since he was a teenager. He took up such pleasant diversions as cricket and snooker while working on remixing tracks for the *Coda* album. His first major appearances were in London on September 20 and 21, 1983, when he played alongside Eric Clapton and Jeff Beck at the ARMS charity show, watched by the Prince and Princess of Wales. He jammed with Clapton and Beck, and played some themes from *Death Wish 2* as well as a moving instrumental version of 'Stairway To Heaven', backed by Simon Phillips on drums. A roar went up as soon as he ventured on stage clad in a grey-striped suit, clutching a Fender Telecaster, and with a cigarette drooping from his lower lip.

Page told me later: "Playing with Eric Clapton and Jeff Beck on the ARMS show was great... brilliant. If

only we'd had more time! It was very emotional when I played 'Stairway To Heaven.' I assumed Jeff Beck was going to come out and help me by playing the melody, but he didn't come on. I'd got the double neck guitar on and everyone was assuming I was gonna play 'Stairway', so I was really in it, I just had to go for it. I saw the video afterwards and saw my face all screwed up. My God. But I was playing for my life."

When the ARMS show went to America Page found himself playing to big, enthusiastic audiences, which further helped restore his confidence. One of the guests on the tour was singer Paul Rodgers (ex-Free, and Bad Company). Rogers and Page began writing songs together which led to the creation of a new band, The Firm. Page also worked with his old folk singer friend Roy Harper. They wrote some material together, recorded an album called 'Whatever Happened To Jugula' (1985) and in August, 1984 they played at the Cambridge Folk Festival with a band that included future Firm member, Tony Franklin, on bass. Page and Harper also appeared on the BBC TV show

The Old Grey Whistle Test. It was a period when Page's guitar technique seemed to have slipped into reverse. Out of practice and sometimes nervous, he seemed to lack the fire that had once been his *forté*. But extensive rehearsals and touring with his new band The Firm, featuring Paul Rodgers, soon brought his guitar playing back up to scratch. The line-up included Tony Franklin (bass), and Chris Slade (drums), and their first album *The Firm* was released on Atlantic in February 1985. The band made its first appearances in Stockholm on November 29, 1984, followed by dates in Germany in December. Incredibly the band had a problem selling tickets in Copenhagen and Frankfurt as nobody knew anything about The Firm, mainly because their album hadn't been released, and a lot of the audience were American servicemen.

Page felt that making the album and forming the band had given him his confidence back, and he certainly played with energy and fire on 'The Chase', an instrumental number on which he featured the violin bow. However, his future plans were not limited to The Firm:

"It started off as a one-off project but now we've seen how it's gone down, who knows? I've got so many projects. The ARMS thing did me the world of good. You can't imagine. It gave me so much confidence. I realized people DID want to see me play again. So I thought blow it, I'm not going to let things slip now. I wanted to get out there. The business aspect is a bore, but the music is fun. After Led Zeppelin I just felt really insecure. Absolutely. I was terrified. I guess that's why I played with Roy Harper whenever I could because I knew his stuff and knew him well. With The Firm it was rock'n'roll which I love. Whenever I feel miserable I put on some old rock'n'roll records and feel so much better. It makes the adrenaline rush. Roots music always has that effect on me. When I play a gig it's there for the moment, a thrill lost in time – unless it's bootlegged! The idea is to show people who had had a lot of faith in me that I'll go out and have a go. Believe me, a lot of fans touch your heart. Especially on the ARMS tour, I realized the fans wanted me back. After Zep I just didn't know what to do. I lived

Tony Franklin, Paul Rodgers (centre) and Jimmy with The Firm 1985

in a total vacuum. I didn't know what I was doing. In the end I went to Bali and just thought about things. And I wasn't sitting on the beach because it was the rainy season! I sat in my room thinking. Then I thought 'dammit I'm going to do The Firm and see if it works.' At this time in my life I should really just do what I enjoy. I used the violin bow in The Firm again because it's fun and I know everyone in the audience enjoys it. Show-manship is great. I've always gone to concerts to be entertained."

> **" LED ZEPPELIN WAS THE SORT OF BAND EVERYONE DREAMS ABOUT. FOR ME IT WAS SUCH AN HONOUR TO BE PART OF IT. "**
>
> JIMMY PAGE

By the mid-80s Jimmy Page had recovered his nerve, was rebuilding his guitar technique and seemed very confident about his future plans. But would he work with Robert Plant again? "I see Robert a lot and we talk a lot and we're good mates still. Sure I'd love to work with Robert again but God knows what sort of musical vehicle we'd be in. He's great. I know him inside out. That's the point. After all those years together you can't help but know each other inside, otherwise you'd have no sensitivity. When you see his big smile – at the end of the day, that's what it's all about." Like Plant, Page looked back on the Led Zeppelin legacy of albums with pride.

"I'm not ashamed of any of that. Led Zeppelin was magic for me. It was a privilege to play in that band. It would have been wrong for me to go out playing the same material and worse to get a singer in to sing all Robert's songs. It would have been morally wrong. I knew that Bonzo wanted that music to go on forever. When I played long solos with Led Zeppelin there was a lot of excitement and I got carried away. Now we keep everything to the point. I used to waffle sometimes in the past. Well, one thing the critics got wrong. If they didn't think we played with conviction they were damn wrong. They say everyone over 30 is finished, which will be fun when they get to 30 by the way. I feel sorry for people who only ever listen to one type of music. When I started playing guitar I got involved in all sorts of music and people; listened to everything from Ravi Shankar to Jimi Hendrix. I thought it was a brilliant time. I feel sorry about the way the scene has changed but who am I to say?

People put me down for what I've done in the past. So I'm waiting for them to be a bit adventurous. Led Zeppelin was the sort of band everyone dreams about. For me it was such an honour to be part of it. I always thought that John Bonham was the most underrated musician ever. He got such power out of his drums. As he got bigger and bigger kits, I had to get bigger amps! I used to play three hour sets every night with Led Zeppelin but I don't think I could get through that now. Once I came off the road after Zeppelin it was such a major part of me missing. I had no vehicle to play in and I had such a reputation for playing live that I got frightened about doing it. If I did four bad gigs, nobody would want to know and I had a few more things I wanted to say in music. So now I'm past middle age. But what do you do when you get to middle age? The music press say you are fucked after you are 30. But I'm not and there's a lot more for me to do."

After playing British shows, including the Hammersmith Odeon, London, The Firm went to America where they were warmly received. The tour climaxed at Madison Square Garden, New York in April, 1985. They even had a hit single from the album called 'Radioactive', and *The Firm* went gold. The band returned to England to play some major venues including Birmingham's NEC and the London Wembley Arena on May 22. The shows weren't sell outs but at Wembley the fans cheered the return of their hero and a new generation got to see a living legend in action. Then, just as Plant and Page were about to make separate tours of the States, came the invitation to play as Led Zeppelin on *Live Aid*. It wasn't what they'd planned, but cajoled by an enthusiastic Bob Geldof, what else could they do? Page, Plant and John Paul Jones played 'Rock And Roll', 'Stairway To Heaven', and 'Whole Lotta Love', for old times sake, and a huge wave of affection greeted the band. Phil Collins jetted across the Atlantic on Concorde to sit in on drums alongside Tony Thompson. As it turned out it wasn't a particularly happy occasion for Collins who had no chance to rehearse and came on stage cold, without any idea what they were going to play.

"I was on tour with my band in America while *Live Aid* was being set up," Collins commented. "Sting rang and asked me to do something with him vocally. But I wanted to play drums with somebody too. There was nobody in England I could play drums with. My manager Tony Smith explained to me it was possible with

Opposite:

"You remember laughter?" Plant and Page reunited at last

The Zeppelin spirit revived at Jason Bonham's wedding, with Bonham Jnr on drums

Concorde to go to America and play there as well. I met Robert Plant in Dallas when he was rehearsing there. Robert said he'd like to do something on *Live Aid* and wouldn't it be great to get Jimmy involved and do a few Zeppelin songs? I said I'd love to play with him and Jimmy – it would be great. That's how it developed. So I did the English part of the show with Sting which was over very quickly. I played some bum notes on the piano and he played some bum notes on the guitar and sang the wrong words. It seemed like magic on the day but when you watch it on video you think 'Oh no!' I got a helicopter from Wembley to Heathrow, got on Concorde and flew to Kennedy. I took another helicopter to Philadelphia which took almost as long as Concorde, then I got a van to the gig, arrived just in time and checked my drums. I went to see Eric Clapton in his dressing room and he said he was playing 'White Room' and 'Layla' and then I went to Robert's dressing room and said 'What are you playing?' They said 'Stairway To Heaven', 'Whole Lotta Love', and 'Rock And Roll.' Well there was a blot on the copy book after

that. First I went on stage and played with Eric and did my songs, then I played with Led Zeppelin, and at the end of it, I was like in a daze. Then I got the last helicopter back to New York and the Concorde home. The Zeppelin performance was a kind of funny experience. Tony Thompson was playing drums too and had rehearsed with Zeppelin. Obviously they hadn't played together for years and there was a lot on the line. It was the Zeppelin revival! I said I couldn't rehearse because I'd been out on tour and then did *Live Aid*. I had been on tour for five months.

"Anyway, I got together with them in the dressing room, with Jimmy, John Paul Jones, Robert and Tony Thompson and I had the funny feeling of being the new boy. Now Tony is a great drummer but when you are playing with two drummers you have to have a certain attitude. You have to back off and not have so much ego and play as a unit. Tony didn't seem to want to do that and within five minutes of me being on stage I felt 'Get me out of here.' It was just weird. If you are playing straight time one of the drummers can't start doing triplet fills 'cos it will start sounding real messy. That was going on and speeding up and slowing down. It wasn't particularly enjoyable and because I hadn't rehearsed and because I'd flown across the Atlantic, Robert laid a lot of the blame at my door, whereas in fact I was trying to play as little as possible to get out of everybody's way. He thought I was tired. But I knew what they wanted. John Bonham was one of my favourite drummers. I grew up watching Zeppelin from their first gig at the Marquee. 'Whole Lotta Love' was a bit chaotic because they can rehearse until they are blue in the face but at the crucial moment they will do what they want to do. Jimmy was feeding back and getting his violin bow out – it was all a bit peculiar. Nice place to visit, but I wouldn't want to live there!" Said Jimmy Page later: "It was a bit of a kamikaze stunt. We only had an hour's rehearsal, but the spirit was there and it was the right time to have a get together."

Robert Plant talked about the reunion a couple of years later, in 1988. "Oh no – it was bloody awful. I was hoarse and Pagey was out of tune. Phil Collins wasn't even at the rehearsal which was painfully evident, but not his fault. We came on as ramshackle as ever, and when I look at the video now I laugh my head off. One-and-a-half billion people and I'm hoarse and Pagey's out of tune and the whole thing is all over the place. So typical. And the roar of the crowd. They were all shouting for Zeppelin. I don't know if I'll ever get over the fact that I don't think I should ever have been a part of it, because it really just stirred the whole thing up again. I went back on my own solo tour a couple of nights later and my voice was perfect. *Live Aid* was a fine cause but it was breaking my word to myself to play there. I mean I'll play with Jimmy forever at one-off occasions in the future, but people watching *Live Aid* thought they were seeing Led Zeppelin and they weren't. It was nowhere near Led Zeppelin. If Bonzo had been there the whole thing would have gelled and it would have been stunningly good. It just goes to show even two drummers couldn't bring it home. It was such a big wire emotionally for me. I don't think I got over it for weeks. The expectations in the air and people weeping at the side of the stage. It showed how many people over the world had been touched by the Zeppelin experience, and I'm rather proud of that."

After the 1986 concert Led Zeppelin did attempt a permanent reunion although it was kept completely under wraps at the time. Tony Thompson came to England for some rehearsals with the three Zep men but got involved in a car crash in Bath and Plant decided he didn't want to pursue the idea any further. While Plant was touring with some success, Page's band, The Firm, released one more album *The Firm Mean Business* in April 1986, then rested for a while before being quietly disbanded after one more US tour. The Firm had played some good music but just lacked the sparkle of its rather more innovative predecessor. Paul Rodgers went off to form a new group with drummer Kenny Jones and Page eventually formed a better band with Jason Bonham, now in his twenties and proving to be an excellent drummer in his own right. Jason Bonham had actually played with Led Zeppelin at Knebworth in 1979 during a sound check. Jimmy Page was out front listening to the sound balance and hadn't realized it was Jason and not his father behind the kit. Jason Bonham contributed to the next Zeppelin reunion held at the Atlantic Records fortieth birthday celebrations in New York – there was no second drummer this time. It was his performance at this gig that led to his being invited to play with Page's new band. Page wasn't too happy with his own performance under the harsh glare of publicity at Madison Square Garden, scene of many past triumphs.

"That wasn't much fun at all. The rehearsals were fabulous. For the show itself we were supposed to play at a particular time and I usually pace myself towards doing something and we were taken from the hotel we were staying in to another hotel near Madison Square. We were ready, expecting to play within thirty minutes. Robert was already there because he had done his set and then we were kept waiting for two-and-a-half hours and I just got more and more nervous. Then the monitors weren't working properly and my gear sounded like crap and unfortunately it wasn't the best of performances. It was a shame really because one wanted to make amends for the frantic set that was done at *Live Aid*."

Page released his first solo album, *Outrider* (Geffen) in June, 1988, but it proved something of a disappointment. Page's new band, with Jason Bonham, included John Miles (vocals) and Durban Laverde (bass), and they were much better live. They began a tour of the States starting at Atlanta, Georgia on September 6, 1988. Page said later: "Jason is coming on very well indeed. It's funny, he knows the Led Zeppelin tracks better than I do! When we did the reunion thing at Madison Square he remembered every note and every phrase that we had played on things like 'The Song Remains The Same' from the recorded version, while we remembered them from the last time we played them on the last European tour, when we had changed them all around. It was fun and very interesting. His father John was the greatest rock drummer ever as far as I'm concerned and Jason was obviously taught by his father and he has the same approach to the bass drum for example, and he has the same intensity. He's developing all the time and using sampling stuff with his kid drums. So he had the greatest teacher in the world and is growing with the music."

Looking back over the post-Zeppelin years Page could see how he had been developing during the 80s. "It took me a long while to embark on a solo career and as it is a solo career I thought I'd start off going back to the roots on the first album and then move in another direction." After touring with Jimmy Page, Jason Bonham later formed his own group simply called Bonham and in March 1989 released his debut album *The Disregard Of Time Keeping*, followed by a full US tour. During the 90s the legacy of Led Zeppelin still loomed large over the founding musicians and the hunger for more music from the source seemed unabated. Page and Plant made a tantalising appearance when they sang three Zeppelin numbers at Knebworth Silver Clef concert on June 30, 1990, among a host of other stars that included Eric Clapton. Asked if Led Zeppelin would ever reform Page simply replied: "You'll have to ask Robert. I love playing that stuff. It's part of me."

In 1993 Led Zeppelin fans were thrown into turmoil by the news that Jimmy Page was linking up – not with Robert Plant – but with his rival, David Coverdale. Many could not disguise their shock at this scheme, which appeared like a deliberate ploy to

> ## " FOR US IT WAS SIMPLY DO OR DIE. IF IT DIDN'T WORK IT WOULDN'T BE THE END OF THE WORLD. "
>
> DAVID COVERDALE

goad Plant into some sort of response. However, taken on face value, it was also a perfectly logical way to combine two talented performers who seemed to get on well with each other. The result was the heavily promoted *Coverdale Page* album. Rock music's political analysts surmized that the situation was a direct result of Plant turning down, in 1990, Page's request for a full Zeppelin reunion, with Jason Bonham on drums. It could have meant millions of dollars for Plant, but he stuck to his principles and refused to join the scheme, leaving Page with the need to find another vocalist. Plant had collaborated with Page on one track on the latter's 1988 *Outrider* solo album, but this had failed to ignite the Zep-style excitement and *Coverdale Page*, with tracks like 'Shake My Tree', 'Over Now', and 'Easy Does It', was much more dynamic. The Zep-inspired riffs gave Page a chance to rock out and Coverdale was given an opportunity to sing his heart out. Coverdale explained that the welcome offer to work with Page came at a difficult stage in his own career. "For us it was simply do or die. If it didn't work it wouldn't be the end of the world. But of course we noticed that enormous expectations were being built up. It was fate that we met. I was in the depths of a personal and musical crisis at the end of 1990 when my Slip Of The Tongue world tour finished. I didn't know if I should continue at all. It was in the following year that I got a 'phone call from an agent who asked me if I was interested in working with Jimmy Page. My first reaction was 'Yes, absolutely.'"

Page had also been faced with a crisis. He had been working on his second solo album and was auditioning singers and becoming increasingly frustrated at the lack of talent displayed. "After listening to the fiftieth demo tape I wanted to pack it in." The agent who brought them together was taking a gamble. Page and Coverdale only really knew each other by sight. Said David: "That's why our first meeting was so important. We had to find out if and how we would get on. We met in New York and after half-an-hour we left the officials and went for a walk in Manhattan. Suddenly we caused a little bit of traffic chaos. Cars stopped and drivers wound down their car windows and asked if we were working together. At that moment we both realized that this was what we owed our audience. We had to present them with a real killer album. That was our only task." Page commented: "After a long time without a record or live presentation, I wanted to make a musical statement and prove that I am still here at my best."

Following the 1992 New York meeting Page went with Coverdale to his home in Lake Tahoe, then they went on to Barbados. Eventually eleven tracks were cut for the *Coverdale Page* CD which was released on March 15, 1993. A full US tour was projected, but in the end Coverdale Page only played some dates at the end of 1993, in Japan. Meanwhile, Plant's US tour went so well it seemed to prove he had taken the right decision. Furthermore, the world had grown weary of speculation and now believed that a reunion would never happen. At which point Robert Plant and Jimmy Page finally decided to get together.

The 1994 release of the *No Quarter: Unledded* (see p130) video and CD, followed by the subsequent hugely successful Page-Plant World Tour of 1995-96 showed that the stalwart rockers meant business. It was a welcome return after many worthy but less exciting projects. Together with young and enthusiastic backing musicians they created valid and intriguing new material, as well as revitalizing many of their greatest hits.

The revival continued three years later when one-time Zep anthem 'Whole Lotta Love' was released and made an appearance in the UK national pop charts. Its September 1997 release represented a major break with tradition for the band. Zeppelin had long fought shy of issuing singles in the UK, yet now Atlantic's release of the dynamic blues classic – first heard on the band's 1969 *Led Zeppelin II* album – came together with a promotional video containing historic archive footage. The special CD single was released on September 1 to support the re-launch of the entire Zeppelin catalogue at mid-price. The 28-year-old performance entered the Top 30, sharing the limelight usually accorded such '90s icons as the Spice Girls and Oasis.

Later in 1997 rumours surfaced that a special anthology video of the band's history was also being assembled, including clips from the historic 1975 Earls Court shows and film of their appearances in Seattle, USA (1977), Bath Festival, England (1970) and at London's Royal Albert Hall (1970).

There was also speculation that Page and Plant might team up with Jason Bonham for a special concert to celebrate the 50th Anniversary of Atlantic Records in March, 1998. Any full scale reunion was being discounted by sources close to the band at the close of 1997, as Jones was busy with his first solo album.

Page and Plant were also working on an album, with producer Steve Albini (of Nirvana and PJ Harvey fame). Several tracks were completed in London in July and September and a spring 1998 release was envisaged.

If 1997 was a full year for Zeppelin fans, the highlight had to be November's eagerly anticipated release of a double CD – *Led Zeppelin: BBC Sessions* – containing Zep performances recorded for radio in 1969 and 1971. It captured the band at their best: young, fresh and bursting with energy. Some 24 tracks displayed scintillating versions of material from their first four studio albums, as well as two songs previously unreleased by the band, Eddie Cochran's 'Something Else', and a version of bluesman Sleepy John Este's, 'The Girl I Love'.

Jimmy Page selected and remastered all the tracks for the two CDs. It was the first official live release from the band since the 1976 soundtrack album from the concert movie *The Song Remains The Same* and it made its debut at number 12 in the US charts. Not bad for a band which had split up more than 17 years earlier!

The CDs benefited from the professional BBC-quality sound engineering of the period, which ensured a real sense of presence and a superb balance. Astonishingly, there were no fillers at all, no routine performances for Zeppelin – every note and every song was meant to count, and it's amusing to hear these blockbusters being accorded polite applause by the attentive British audience.

It was a double-blast from a quartet clearly at their peak, an immensely powerful sound that redefined songs which have become so familiar in their album incarnations. A combination of youthful energy, virility (Plant never loses an opportunity to give his lemon a quick squeeze just to ensure the point is absolutely understood) and awe-inspiring control from all four members of the band, it was a revelatory release with a crystal-clear sound. Thanks to the BBC, it can be 1971 forever for Led Zeppelin fans.

CHRONOLOGY

January 9, 1944
James Patrick Page born Heston, Middlesex, England.

January 31, 1946
John Baldwin (John Paul Jones) born Sidcup, Kent, England.

May 31, 1948
John Henry Bonham born Redditch, Worcestershire, England.

August 20, 1948
Robert Anthony Plant born West Bromwich, Staffordshire, England.

January 1963
Jimmy Page plays guitar on Jet Harris & Tony Meehan's record *Diamonds*.

June 1966
Jimmy Page joins The Yardbirds on bass guitar.

November 1966
Jimmy Page replaces Jeff Beck as lead guitarist for The Yardbirds.

March 1967
John Bonham and Robert Plant both play in The Band Of Joy.

August 1968
Jimmy Page asks Robert Plant to join his band The New Yardbirds.

September 1968
The New Yardbirds rehearse with Jimmy Page (guitar), Robert Plant (vocals), John Paul Jones (bass and organ), and John Bonham (drums).

September 14, 1968
The New Yardbirds make their debut in Copenhagen, Denmark.

October 1968
Led Zeppelin debut album recorded at Olympic Studios, Barnes, England.

October 17, 1968
Band make first appearance billed as Led Zeppelin, at Surrey University, England.

November 1968
Led Zeppelin sign to Atlantic Records.

December 26, 1968
Led Zeppelin play first American show in Boston, Massachussetts, supporting Vanilla Fudge.

January 17, 1969
Led Zeppelin debut album released in America.

March 25, 1969
Band filmed for *Super Session* movie in Staines, England.

June 28, 1969
Led Zeppelin play biggest UK gig to 12,000 fans at Bath Festival, England.

October 17, 1969
Led Zeppelin play at Carnegie Hall, New York.

October 31, 1969
Led Zeppelin II released.

September 17, 1970
Led Zeppelin play Madison Square Garden, New York City.

October 5, 1970
Led Zeppelin III released.

March 5, 1971
First 'Stairway To Heaven' live performance in UK at Ulster Hall, Belfast, Northern Ireland.

November 12, 1971
Four Symbols – Led Zeppelin's fourth album released.

November 30, 1972
100,000 tickets sold in one day for UK tour.

March 26, 1973
Houses Of The Holy – the fifth Led Zeppelin album released.

May 5, 1973
Led Zeppelin play to 56,800 fans at Tampa Stadium, Florida.

July 29, 1973
Band robbed of cash at Drake Hotel, New York City.

May 10, 1974
Led Zeppelin launch own Swan Song label.

February 24, 1975
Physical Graffiti double album released.

May 17, 1975
First of five shows at Earls Court Arena, London, England.

August 4, 1975
Robert Plant seriously injured in car crash in Rhodes, Greece.

April 5, 1976
Seventh album *Presence* released.

October 20, 1976
World premier of Zeppelin movie *The Song Remains The Same*.

April 1, 1977
Zeppelin's eleventh US tour opens in Dallas, Texas.

July 23, 1977
Led Zeppelin entourage involved in a fight backstage at Oakland Coliseum.

July 26, 1977
Death of Robert Plant's son Karac from a stomach infection, in England. Plant returns home and US tour cancelled.

August 4, 1979
Led Zeppelin played first of two shows at Knebworth, Hertfordshire, their last appearance in Britain.

August 20, 1979
In Through The Out Door album released worldwide.

June 17, 1980
Led Zeppelin's last European tour starts at Westfalen Halle, Dortmund, Germany.

July 7, 1980
Led Zeppelin play final show at Eissporthalle, Berlin.

September 25, 1980
John Bonham found dead in bed after drinking bout, at Jimmy Page's home in Windsor, Berkshire.

December 4, 1980
Led Zeppelin announce they will break up.

June 1982
Robert Plant releases first solo album *Pictures At Eleven*.

December, 1982
Release of tenth Led Zeppelin album *Coda* on Swan Song.

September 21, 1983 Jimmy Page plays instrumental version of 'Stairway To Heaven' at London's Royal Albert Hall during ARMS charity show.

March, 1985
Jimmy Page forms The Firm with singer Paul Rodgers and releases album.

July 13, 1985
Led Zeppelin reunion appearance at US Live Aid show held at JFK Stadium, Philadelphia, with Phil Collins on drums.

May 14, 1988
Led Zeppelin with Page, Plant, Jones and Jason Bonham on drums play 'Stairway To Heaven' and 'Whole Lotta Love' at Madison Square Garden, New York for the fortieth anniversary celebration for Atlantic Records.

June 1988
Jimmy Page releases first solo album, *Outrider*.

September 1988
Jimmy Page band with Jason Bonham on drums and John Miles (vocals) tours US.

June 30, 1990
Robert Plant and Jimmy Page perform at Knebworth Festival, Hertfordshire.

October 15, 1990
Remasters (Atlantic) boxed set released in Europe containing twenty-four Led Zeppelin tracks.

October 29, 1990
Boxed set compilation *Led Zeppelin* (Atlantic) containing fifty-four digitally-remastered tracks, is released worldwide.

March, 1993
Coverdale/Page album released featuring Page with David Coverdale (vocals).

September 1993
Led Zeppelin Remastered boxed Set 2 (Atlantic) released.

Autumn 1994
Jimmy Page and Robert Plant reunite to record 90 minute MTV Special *No Quarter – Unledded*.

February 26, 1995
Plant/Page embark on American leg of extensive world tour.

June 6, 1995
Page/Plant start European tour dates in Paris, France.

June 25, 1995
Page/Plant play Glastonbury Festival, England.

July 25, 1995
Plant/Page play at Wembley Arena, London, England. Led Zeppelin's manager Peter Grant visits the show.

November 21, 1995
Death of Peter Grant aged 60.

Spring 1997
Plant/Page start work on new album and plan 1998 second world tour.

Summer 1997
Plant and Page work on new album.

September 1997
'Whole Lotta Love' released as single.

November 1997
BBC Sessions released.

DISCOGRAPHY

Led Zeppelin (1969)
Atlantic Records K 40031 Cas K 440031
CD K 240031
Good Times Bad Times, Babe I'm Gonna
Leave You, You Shook Me, Dazed And
Confused, Your Time Is Gonna Come, Black
Mountain Side, Communication Breakdown, I
Can't Quit You Baby, How Many More Times

Led Zeppelin II (1969)
Atlantic Records K 40037 Cas K 440037
CD K 240037
Whole Lotta Love, What Is And What Should
Never Be, The Lemon Song, Thank You,
Heartbreaker, Livin' Lovin' Maid (She's Just
A Woman), Ramble On, Moby Dick, Bring It
On Home

Led Zeppelin III (1970)
Atlantic Records K 50002 Cas K 450002
CD K 250 002
Immigrant Song, Friends, Celebration Day,
Since I've Been Loving You, Out On The Tiles,
Gallows Pole, Tangerine, That's The Way,
Bron-Y-Aur Stomp, Hats Off To (Roy) Harper

Four Symbols (1971)
Atlantic Records K 50008 Cas K 450008
CD 250 008
Black Dog, Rock And Roll, The Battle Of
Evermore, Stairway To Heaven, Misty
Mountain Hop, Four Sticks, Going To
California, When The Levee Breaks

Houses Of The Holy (1973)
Atlantic Records K 50014 Cas K 450014
CD 250 014
The Song Remains The Same, The Rain Song,
Over The Hills And Far Away, The Crunge,
Dancing Days, D'yer Mak'er, No Quarter, The
Ocean

Physical Graffiti (1975)
Swan Song Records SSK 89400 Cas SK4
89400 CD SK 289400
Custard Pie, The Rover, In My Time Of Dying,
Houses Of The Holy, Trampled Underfoot,
Kashmir, In The Light, Bron-Yr-Aur, Down By
The Seaside, Ten Years Gone, Night Flight,
The Wanton Song, Boogie With Stu, Black
Country Woman, Sick Again

The Song Remains The Same (1976)
Swan Song Records SSK 89402 Cas SK4
89402 CD SK 289402
Rock And Roll, Celebration Day, The Song
Remains The Same, Rain Song, Dazed And
Confused, No Quarter, Stairway To Heaven,
Moby Dick, Whole Lotta Love

Presence (1976)
Swan Song Records SSK 59402 Cas SK4
59402 CD SK 259402
Achilles Last Stand, For Your Life, Royal
Orleans, Nobody's Fault But Mine, Candy
Store Rock, Hots On For Nowhere, Tea
For One

In Through The Out Door (1979)
Swan Song Records SSK 59410 Cas SK4
59410 CD SK 259410
In The Evening, South Bound Saurez, Fool In
The Rain, Hot Dog, Carouselambra, All My
Love, I'm Gonna Crawl

Coda (1982)
Swan Song Record 79005-1 CD 790 051-2
We're Gonna Groove, Poor Tom, I Can't Quit
You Baby, Walter's Walk, Ozone Baby,
Darlene, Bonzo's Montreaux, Wearing And
Tearing

Led Zeppelin (1990)
Atlantic Records 6 LP Box 7567-82144-1 4
CD Box CD 7567-82144-2
Whole Lotta Love, Heartbreaker,
Communication Breakdown, Babe I'm Gonna
Leave You, What Is And What Should Never
Be, Thank You, I Can't Quit You Baby, Dazed
And Confused, Your Time Is Gonna Come,
Ramble On, Travelling Riverside Blues,
Friends, Celebration Day, Hey Hey What Can I
Do, White Summer/Black Mountain Side,
Black Dog, Over The Hills And Far Away,
Immigrant Song, The Battle Of Evermore,
Bron-Y-Aur Stomp, Tangerine, Going To
California, Since I've Been Loving You, D'yer
Mak'er, Gallows Pole, Custard Pie, Misty
Mountain Hop, Rock And Roll, The Rain
Song, Stairway To Heaven, Kashmir,
Trampled Underfoot, For Your Life, No
Quarter, Dancing Days, When The Levee
Breaks, Achilles Last Stand, The Song
Remains The Same, Ten Years Gone, In My
Time Of Dying, In The Evening, Candy Store
Rock, The Ocean, Ozone Baby, Houses Of
The Holy, Wearing And Tearing, Poor Tom,
Nobody's Fault But Mine, Fool In The Rain, In
The Light, The Wanton Song, Moby
Dick/Bonzo's Montreaux, I'm Gonna Crawl,
All My Love

Remasters 1 (1990)
3 LPs Atlantic 7567-80415-1 2 CDs Atlantic
7567 80415-2
Communication Breakdown, Babe I'm Gonna
Leave You, Good Times Bad Times, Dazed
And Confused, Whole Lotta Love,
Heartbreaker, Ramble On, Immigrant Song,
Celebration Day, Since I've Been Loving You,
Black Dog, Rock And Roll, The Battle Of
Evermore, Misty Mountain Hop, Stairway To

Heaven, The Song Remains The Same, The
Rain Song, D'yer Mak'er, No Quarter, Houses
Of The Holy, Kashmir, Trampled Under Foot,
Nobody's Fault But Mine, Achilles Last Stand,
All My Love, In The Evening

Remasters 2 (1990)
CD Atlantic 7567 82144 2
Whole Lotta Love, Heartbreaker,
Communication Breakdown, Babe I'm Gonna
Leave You, Dazed And Confused, Ramble
On, Your Time Is Gonna Come, What Is And
What Should Never Be, Thank You, I Can't
Quit You Baby, Friends, Celebration Day,
Travelling Riverside Blues, Hey Hey What
Can I Do, White Summer, Black
Mountainside, Black Dog, Over The Hills And
Far Away, Immigrant Song, The Battle Of
Evermore, Bron-y-Aur Stomp, Tangerine,
Going To California, Since I've Been Loving
You, D'yer Mak'er, Gallows Pole, Custard
Pie, Misty Mountain Hop, Rock And Roll, The
Rain Song, Stairway To Heaven, Kashmir,
Trampled Underfoot, For Your Life, No
Quarter, Dancing Days, When The Levee
Breaks, The Song Remains The Same,
Achilles Last Stand, Ten Years Gone, Candy
Store Rock, Moby Dick, In My Time Of Dying,
In The Evening, The Ocean, Ozone Baby,
Houses Of The Holy, Wearing And Tearing,
Poor Tom, Nobody's Fault But Mine, Fool In
The Rain, In The Light, The Wanton Song,
I'm Gonna Crawl, All My Love

Led Zeppelin Boxed Set 2 (1993)
Atlantic CDs 7567 82477-2
Good Times Bad Times, We're Gonna Groove,
Night Flight, That's The Way, Baby Come On
Home, The Lemon Song, You Shook Me, Boogie
With Stu, Bron-Yr-Aur, Down By The Seaside,
Out On The Tiles, Black Mountain Side, Moby
Dick, Sick Again, Hot Dog, Carouselambra,
South Bound Saurez, Walter's Walk, Darlene,
Black Country Woman, How Many More Times,
The Rover, Four Sticks, Hats Off To (Roy)
Harper, I Can't Quit You Baby, Hots On For
Nowhere, Livin' Lovin' Maid (She's Just A
Woman), Royal Orleans, Bonzo's Montreaux,
The Crunge, Bring It On Home, Tea For One

**The Complete Studio Recordings Of
Led Zeppelin** (1993)
Atlantic 7825 26/2
Nine original album titles on ten CDs. All re-
mastered except for 'The Song Remains The
Same'

BBC Sessions (November 1997)
Atlantic Records
You Shook Me; I Can't Quit You Baby;
Communication Breakdown; Dazed And

Confused; The Girl I Love She Got Long Black Wavy Hair; What Is And What Should Never Be; Communication Breakdown; Travelling Riverside Blues; Whole Lotta Love; Somethin' Else; Communication Breakdown; I Can't Quit You Baby; You Shook Me; How Many More Times; Immigrant Song; Heartbreaker; Since I've Been Loving You; Black Dog; Dazed And Confused; Stairway To Heaven; Going To California; That's The Way; Whole Lotta Love (medley): Boogie Chillun'/Fixin' To Die/That's Alright Mama/A Mess Of Blues; Thank You

LED ZEPPELIN SINGLES (US Release only)
March 1969 Good Times, Bad Times.
Communication Breakdown
Atlantic 2614

November 1969 Whole Lotta Love/Livin' Lovin' Maid
Atlantic 2690

November 1970 Immigrant Song/Hey Hey What Can I Do
Atlantic 2777

December 1971 Black Dog/Misty Mountain Hop
Atlantic 2849

March 1972 Rock And Roll/Four Sticks
Atlantic 2865

May 1973 Over The Hills And Far Away/Dancing Days
Atlantic 2970

October 1973 D'yer Mak'er/The Crunge
Atlantic 2986

March 1975 Trampled Underfoot/Black Country Woman
Swan Song 70102

May 1976 Candy Store Rock/Royal Orleans
Swan Song 70110

December 1979 Fool In The Rain/Hot Dog
Swan Song 71003

September 1997 (and UK release)
Whole Lotta Love

SOLO ALBUMS

JOHN PAUL JONES
1985 **Scream For Help**
Atlantic 780 190-1
Spaghetti Junction, Bad Child, Take It Or Leave It, Chilli Sauce, Silver Train, Christie, Here I Am, When You Fall In Love, Crackback

JIMMY PAGE
1982 **Death Wish II** (Original Soundtrack)
Swan Song SSK 59415
Who's To Blame, The Chase, City Sirens, Jam Sandwich, Carole's Theme, The Release,

Hotel Rats & Photostats, Shadow In The City, Jill's Theme, Prelude, Big Bad Sax & Violence, Hypnotising Ways

1985 **The Firm**
Atlantic 781 239-1 CD 781 239-2
Closer, Make Or Break, Someone To Love, Together, Radioactive, You've Lost That Lovin' Feeling, Money Can't Buy, Satisfaction Guaranteed, Midnight Moonlight

1985 **Harper & Page: Whatever Happened To Jugula?**
Beggars Banquet BEHA 60
Nineteen Forty-Eightyish, Bad Speech, Hope, Hangman, Elizabeth, Frozen Moment, Twentieth Century Man, Advertisement

1986 **The Firm Mean Business**
Atlantic 781 628-1 CD 781 628-2
Fortune Hunter, Cadillac, All The Kings Horses, Live In Peace, Tear Down The Walls, Dreaming, Free To Live, Spirit Of Love

1988 **Jimmy Page: Outrider**
Geffen WX 155 924 188-1 CD 9241882
Wasting My Time, Wanna Make Love, Writes Of Winter, The Only One, Liquid Mercury, Hummingbird, Emerald Eyes, Prison Blues, Blues Anthem

ROBERT PLANT
1982 **Pictures At Eleven**
Swan Song SSK 594 18 CD SK 259418
Burning Down One Side, Moonlight In Samosa, Pledge Pin, Slow Dancer, Worse Than Detroit, Fat Lip, Like I've Never Been Gone, Mystery Title

1983 **The Principle Of Moments**
Es Paranza 790-101 CD 790 101-2
Other Arms, In The Mood, Messin' With The Mekon, Wreckless Love, Thru' With The Two Step, Horizontal Departure, Stranger Here Than Over There, Big Log

1984 **The Honeydrippers Volume 1**
Es Paranza 790 220-1
I Get A Thrill, Sea Of Love, Got A Woman, Young Boy Blues, Rockin' At Midnight

1985 **Shaken 'n' Stirred**
Es Paranza 790 265-1 CD 790 265-2
Hip To Hoo, Kallalou Kallalou, Too Loud, Trouble Your Money, Pink and Black, Little By Little, Doo Doo A Do Do, Easily Lead, Sixes and Seven

1988 **Now And Zen**
Atlantic 790 863-1 CD 790 863-2
Heaven Knows, Dance On My Own, Tall Cool One, The Way I Feel, Helen Of Troy, Billy's Revenge, Ship Of Fools, Why, White Clean And Neat

1990 **Manic Nirvana**
Es Paranza WX 339 CD Atlantic WX 339CD
Hurting Kind (I've Got My Eyes On You), Big Love, S S S & Q, I Cried, Nirvana, Tie Dye On The Highway, Your Ma Said You Cried In Your

Sleep Last Night, Anniversary, Liars Dance, Watching You,

1993 **Fate Of Nations**
Fontana 514867/2
Calling To You, Down To The Sea, Come Into My Life, I Believe, 29 Palms, Memory Song (Hello, Hello), If I Were A Carpenter, Colours Of A Shade, Promised Land, The Greatest Gift, Great Spirit, Network News

DAVID COVERDALE and JIMMY PAGE
1993 **Coverdale Page**
EMI 07777 81401 22
Shake My Tree, Waiting On You, Take Me For A Little While, Pride And Joy, Over Now, Feeling Hot, Easy Does It, Take A Look At Yourself, Don't Leave Me This Way, Absolution Blues, Whisper A Prayer For The Dying

JIMMY PAGE and ROBERT PLANT
1994 **Page & Plant: No Quarter**
Fontana 526 362-2
Nobody's Fool But Mine, Thank You, No Quarter, Friends, Yallah, City Don't Cry, Since I've Been Loving You, The Battle Of Evermore, Wonderful One, Wah Wah, That's The Way, Gallows Pole, Four Sticks, Kashmir

PICTURE CREDITS

The publishers would like to thank the following sources for their kind permission to reproduce the pictures in this book:

Camera Press Ltd./Wolfgang Heilemann
Corbis UK Ltd.
Mary Evans Picture Library
Robert Harding Picture Library/Gavin Hellier
Hulton Getty
London Features International/K.Callahan, Simon Fowler, Jan Goedfroit, Frank Griffen, Peter Mazel, Ilpo Musto, Michael Putland, G Tucker
Mirror Syndication International
Pictorial Press/Bodnar, Jordan, Seymour, Van Houten, Rob Verhorst, Vinyl
Relay Photos/Justin Thomas
Redferns/ Richie Aaron, Dick Barnatt, Chuck Boyd, Fin Costello, Ian Dickson, James Bizi Dittiger, Mick Gold, William Gottlieb/Library of Congress, Tom Hanley, Michael Ochs Archive, Mike Prior, David Redfern, Ebert Roberts, Graham Wiltshire
Retna/G. Hankeroot/Sunshine, Photofest, Neal Preston, Michael Putland, Luciano Viti
S.I.N.
Topham Picturepoint/Warners

Every effort has been made to acknowledge correctly and contact the source and/copyright holder of each picture, and Carlton Books Limited apologises for any unintentional errors or omissions which will be corrected in future editions of this book.

INDEX